A Different World

Ashwell before 1939

Albert Sheldrick

Cortney Publications

DEDICATION

I am pleased to dedicate this book
to my dear wife Winnie,
who has looked after me so well,
in sickness and in health,
for over half a century.

ISBN 0 904378 37 3

Published by Cortney Publications,
57 Ashwell Street, Ashwell, Baldock, Herts.

Cover design by Colin Barker (Ashwell)
Word processing by Judith Catterick (Ashwell)
Page preparation by Forest Publication Services (Luton)
Reproduction film by Monographics (Dunstable)
Printing and Binding by
Woolnough Bookbinding Ltd. (Irthlingborough)

Contents

Note concerning the photographs
The photographs are broadly divided into groups illustrating a particular subject – Schools, Streets, Shops, Advertisements, Churches, Transport, Unique Sights and Events, Leisure Activities, Documents, Characters, Farming, Brewing, Pubs, and finally The Museum.

Where possible we have put names to faces and the date (sometimes approximate) of the photograph. Please let us know of any errors or omissions so they can be rectified in any future editions. Credit to the photograph donor is given in the caption, in brackets.

Preface

"A fair town Aescewell, now Ashwell. The River Rhee issues from a source of springs shaded on every side with tall ashes." So wrote Sir Henry Chauncy in his Historical Antiquities of Hertfordshire published in 1700. The water is so clear and cold "that it gripes horses not used to drink it," Salmon, another historian, remarks.

But this is not a History of Ashwell. Albert Sheldrick is not a professional historian: he is an eye witness. The main thrust of this book is the Ashwell of the 1920s and 30s.

But he has an eye for the past, and he leads us into the twentieth century with strands from the past which had such a vital influence on the Ashwell in which he grew up and which he is uniquely equipped to write about.

It is local history with a difference, full of humour and humanity, much of it observed through the eyes of the schoolboy, later bricklayer cum honorary museum curator, who would probably have gone to university nowadays. There are many delightful snippets.

The war to end all wars was over. It was the dawn of a new era. The first motor car, the doctor's, appeared in the village and the first farm tractor. A versatile Cockney hat manufacturer came and, amid much speculation and gossip, built the first bus - "Ye Olde Tin Can".

Tucked away in a corner of North Hertfordshire, Ashwell was in many ways any large village at this time: richer perhaps in history, more full of character than most, and certainly with its fair share of "characters". Also it was endowed with an amazing range of crafts and skills, and shops that supplied almost every need. If you couldn't buy it, somebody else could make it.

Every Monday morning Mr Hibbert, the sweep, trudged six miles over the fields from Arlesey, brush and brass-capped rods on his shoulder, to sweep Ashwell chimneys at sixpence a time. Black as the ace of spades. he would trudge back again at the end of the day.

In summer, beneath the skylarks' canopy of song, the rolling expanse of cornfields were scarlet with poppies and golden with charlock ("carlocks" everybody called them), brighter than the more subdued red and yellow of sainfoin and trefoil of the hayfields. In winter, when snow lay crisp and even, farm workers set snares, baited with raisins soaked in brandy or whisky, to tempt these tiny larks to end up as an expensive luxury served in the best London hotels. For themselves, men netted sparrows roosting under thatched eaves for next day's sparrow pie. And Joe Man served up to his friends a special line in snail suppers.

From his perch beside a chimneystack, or with his ear to the ground on an inside job, or gawping as a boy in the shops - and what shops, and what service! - Albert missed little. For many, life was hard and unyielding and working hours were long. But looking back benignly with Albert, we can see there was fun.

Robert Christy

Acknowledgements

We are indebted to many people for their help and encouragement in publishing this book. Those who have lent us their treasured photographs are deeply appreciated. Special thanks are due to Robert Godsman and Peter Greener – their collections of Ashwell Postcards have been invaluable; to the Day, Bryant and Howes families, Mrs Alison Stafford, Mrs Bessie Wallace, Mr & Mrs H. Bullard and the Ashwell Further Education Centre for their contributions; to Oliver Woodforde, son of Ashwell's Doctor from 1900-1933, whose History of Ashwell and photographs have been most useful. Some pictures we have been able to reproduce by courtesy of the Comet Series of Weekly Newspapers, a member of the Home Counties Newspaper Group. Two farming photographs supplied by TV Personality Richard Whitmore are of exceptional interest, as is that loaned by Mr & Mrs B. Northern. Mrs Berry unearthed a rare photograph of Mrs Wolverley Fordham, and the author himself supplied quite a few others. Photographs by T.B. Latchmore, Doris and George Shelton, who had such keen eyes for the beauties of our village, whose work has been carried on so ably by Philip Coverdale, have been included. To all these we are most grateful.

Above all, this book's unique assembly of photographs, sketches and documents would have been impossible without the Museum's collection, to which many have contributed. Many photographs have been enhanced by the skilled work of Ian and Sue Walters, and Monographics Ltd. of Dunstable have not only used the latest laser scanning techniques, but have speedily produced quality film from which the printing plates have been made.

The author would like to specially thank Robery Christy and Arthur Scholfield for their editorial work, and the former for his Preface; Philip Crump, Howard Day, Kevan Morrison and David Short for their interest and encouragement; Judith Catterick who patiently word-processed and re-processed the text; Barry Yeomans of Forest Publication Services for his expertise in page layout; Norman Gurney, who has not only burned the midnight oil but has left no stone unturned in seeking out this wonderful collection of Ashwell and Ashwell folks to publish this unique book.

We apologise in advance for any errors and omissions – we will endeavour to correct these in any future edition.

Cortney Publications

Introduction

Among the account books and documents left by her father, the late John Sale of Farrows Farm, Mrs Bessie Wallace found a hand-written document undated and unsigned. It was headed "A description of Ashwell Parish more than fifty years ago by an old Merchant Taylors pupil. Z.H.L."

It was written about 1840. Parts of it are indecipherable and often ungrammatical.

The Village, roads and nooks, also the lands in occupation, Farms. Comprising High St. Back St commonly called Old Tommy Westropes and Old Tom Chapmans Backsides. Streets leading out of High Street etc. Lucas Lane, right and left of Spring head, Limekiln Lane, Three Tuns yard, Hoddle, Bulls Head Alley, Edwards Lane, Workhouse Lane to Carters Pond and the Mill Street; Bear Lane, Dovehouse Lane and at Black Phil Waldocks, the ... Nook.

What I have to say about the land, I will commence upon the Inner Circle of the Parish, which will be close to where the water rises out of the chalk.

Melbourne's Close, Bacon's. Footpath pieces, Prissons, Richardsons acre, Chapman's Bank closes, Hunts close, Thompson's orchard, Chapman's orchard, Tommy Westrope's Quaker close, Bacon's close, Morice's Pastures. Bailey' close, Hart's barn close, Billy Westrope's close, Tommy Chapman's close, then Morice, Hart's Thomas and Pittys, Edwards eye, Christy's close, Sales, Burr's, Chapman's. Cockcrowing Close and Lawyers close Merchant Taylors orchard, Football Close, Field gates, Weston Wiggs. Cow Lane closes, Ducklake closes, Spring Head pieces, Cage, green and the Churchyard.

The Middle circle. Townsend close, Bacon leg, Bank Pieces, Windmill bit, Workhouse Hill, Partridge Way, Harboro Way, Newnham Way, Caldecote Way. The Willows, Parklane, The meads, Littlefield, Buttway, Prisoms, Elbrook, Common Lane,

The outer circle ... Lees, Paddocks, Baldwyn corner, Ruddery, Redlands Field, Highlow path, Hearty Green, Forty foot way, Baldock hole, Farthing Hab, Footpath hill, Kingsland Way, Springs ditch, Lushway, Kingsland Bottom, Rugsden bottom, Lousy bush, Cat bottom, Bygrave hedges, Bygrave foot, Claybush shot, Claybush way, Partridge way, Long and Short paintrees, Newnham bottom, Greenly Hill Caldecote Hill, Quarry hill, Baccath Fields, Hungrey well, Clackets close, Bullocks, Sunnells and cowpasture, Sansomes, Peeks Lane, Ashwell End closes, Wafers Green, Fanmead, Ley close, Harts Spring, Beanhill. Barresford, Cuckoo spinney, Blocksmead spinney, Pudding furlong, Barnsbury shot, Wisemans close, Fan Shot, Mobs hole, Swans-nest acre, Whitegates, Rules towards. Hooks mill, Old cow common, shots, Brick kiln field. Tinkers close, Vineyard, Upperend mill field, Snakes piece Paddocks close, Baldwyns corner, Ruddery hill, Shire baulk shot, Redland field, Odsey Lane pieces.

Trade and profession and the Manager.

Old Will and Richard Lucas, Ratcachers. William Thompson, Gentleman. Joseph Kirbyshire, Farmer. Ann Bowman, ... and Publican. John Lees, Farmer. John Tottman Chapman, Farmer. Thomas Westrope, Farmer. Billy Bacon, Farmer and Horse Slaughterer. William and Sam Worboys, Farmers & Carriers etc. Abraham Hart, Farmer and Speechmaker. William Westrope, Batchelor Farmer. Thomas Chapman, Farmer & Mary Ball, Lady. John Sale, Farmer. Ousiders, Edward Pain Sen. Richard Westrope,

Farmer & Malster. William Kerbyshire, Farmer. Edward King & Oswald Fordham, Malsters, Brewers & Farmers. Benjamin Christy Sen, Farmed a little grass. Simeon Leete, Farmer. Mobs Hole. Old Rule, Farmer. Joseph Westrope, Farmer. Seth Long, Farmer. Slip End. Spiritual Informers. Revd Henry Morice, Church of England. Revd Richardson, Noncomformist. Other local men. Doctor Woodforde. Doctor Flocton twas other FF(?) for short intervals. John Thomas, Schoolmaster. Martha Hart, Schoolmistress. Sarah Harradine, Schoolmistress. Mrs Bailey, Schoolmistress. Sally Ripshire, Schoolmistress. George Garrod, Tailor. John Westrope, Grocer & Draper. George Christy, Grocer & Draper. William Edwards, Grocer & Draper. Jonathan Picking, Carpenter. Thomas Picking Sen, Carpenter. Thomas Picking Jun, Carpenter. Old Kitchener and John, Butchers. Old Simonce, Butcher. Old Castle, Butcher. Jim Gentle, Butcher. John Strickland & Sons, Shoemakers. Jabez Richardson, Shoemaker. Tom Flitton, Brewer at Fordhams. W. Brick, Farm Bailiff at Fordhams. Mrs Gunner, Yeast Retailer. Old Pitty, Miller for J.G. Fordham. Allen Flitton, Miller at Stump mill J.G. Fordhams. William Kitchener, Miller at smock mill. William Pack, Blacksmith. John & Jim Pack, Blacksmiths. Tiddle whop Gentle, Blacksmith. Charles Bonnett, Fruit buyer & clothes repairer. John Carter, Barber & clock repairer. George Bird, Publican Bulls Head. William Flint, Publican Rose & Crown, Quack Doctor etc. Thos Worboys, Publican Bushel & Strike. Mr Roberts, Exiseman. Sam Thorne, Wheelwright. Abram Thorne, Wheelwright. James Pitty, Wheelwright. George Pitty, Carrier. Miss Pitty, Dressmaker. Peter Bailey, Bricklayer. Peter Bailey Jun, Bricklayer. Thos Burr, Farmer & Entire Horsekeeper. William Lee, Grass Lane & Farm Bailiff. Old Titmus, Shepherd. Old Gates, Shepherd. Old Harradine, Shepherd. John Ward, Shepherd. Edmund Harradine, Shepherd. Old Tom Wake, Shepherd. William Picket, Shepherd. Samuel Malyon, Shepherd. Old Wil Langham, Shepherd. Timothy Gentle, Herdsman. John Flitton Sen, Church clock & grave digger.

P.S. This history is old to a few. And new to a great many of the present Parishioners. Z.H.L.

Bakers. Butlers & Coachmen omitted. Charles Porter, Old Strickland & Tunnis, Bob Luff & Ted Luff.

In the Ashwell I write about, which mainly concerns the first thirty odd years of this century, many of the names and places re-appear, although by 1939 many have disappeared. I have tried to write about living history and have selected in the earlier part some of the most important events, activities and developments which went into the making of Ashwell before this century. I am not a professional historian. I have written largely as an observer and a collector of facts and artefacts. I have tried to add a little humour, always remembering Schoolmaster Biles' injunction:

"You will find every word you need in the Bible"

Albert Sheldrick

Bricklayer, Builder's Foreman, Museum Founder, Curator and Author

Bridge over the River Rhee in Mill Street: Christmas 1927 (G. Shelton)

The Origins of Ashwell's Name

In the year 1728, N. Salmon, Bachelor of Law, wrote of Ashwell in these words: "It stands upon the source of the River Rhee, which breaks out of the rock in this Vill from many Springs, with such force as to form a stream, remarkable for being clear, and so cold, that it gripes horses not used to drink it. Around the Spring Head grow Ash trees very kindly, which gave occasion to the name. The water bubbles out at as many places and in as great abundance, and in just such a bottom, under a hill, as doth the famous Isis or Thames in Gloucestershire. It quits the County when it goes out of this Parish ...

Sir Henry Chauncey wrote in his Historical Antiquities of Hertfordshire in 1700: "A fair town called Aescewell now Ashwell is situated in the champion (old name for good quality land) on a low ground, upon the river Rhee which issues from a source of Springs that dreins thro small veins out of a Rock of stone, shaded on every side with tall ashes. These Springs the Saxons of old called Wells and hence some think they have named this town Ashwell."

The Rev. Edward Conybeare describes the spring as "the special glory of Ashwell from a semi-circular hollow, shaded by a grove of fine ash trees, gush out springs upon springs of the clearest water. Few rivers in England, or indeed anywhere, can boast so picturesque an origin.

"The ash trees, however, are not, as one is apt to think at first, the origin of the name, but its consequence. The first syllable embodies that Celtic word for water as Axe, Exe, Esk and Usk meet us in so many places all over Great Britain; and this syllable at some far back date, suggested the planting of ashes around the well."

Professor Skeat, on the derivation of the name wrote: "It is Ashes well, or the well of Ashes; there were old charters which mentioned a man named Ashe."

We know from Bede, the Saxon historian, that the Saxons assembled at certain sacred places for the celebration of religious rites. Trees, rocks and wells mark their sacred places, and that these were venerated by the Saxons is not just a matter of conjecture.

J Frederick Hodgetts, who dedicated his book Older England to his friend Ruskin, says, "The giant Ymir had been slain by the sons of Bor, and of the giant's corpse they formed the world. And the universe was an ash tree. In its broadest sense it is the world of nature, and in its less general teaching, man.

"The ash was given a special name, 'the fear shaker', or that which causes men to tremble with awe.

"This myth says its roots are nine in number; the nine roots extend far below the regions known to man, and there they form nine worlds; this region is under the dominion of the goddess Hela, who receives the souls of those not killed in battle, the souls of usurers, cowards, adulterers and those who slay their enemies by unfair means." This region lives with us today, in our word "hell".

Here it is interesting to note that Elbrook Lane, Ashwell, was known 300 years ago as Helabeck Lane. The story continues, "Each root is described. Under the third root is Mimers Well, in which Odin left his eye as a pledge for the deep draught from the waters there, and from this well the roots of the trees are renewed as they are gnawed by the serpent. This typifies the gnawing decay arising from sensuality, by the grovelling serpent. The refreshment of sacred truth brought from the holy well restores the tree".

So it seems that Ashwell stood high in the estimation of our Saxon forefathers, who made pilgrimages from far and near to see the sacred rites of their religion, and better to understand its symbolism at the nine sister spring with the sacred ash about its banks.

The names of the days of the week, most of the Church's great days and holidays, Easter, Yule, Lent, are all derived from these pagan worshippers. Even Odsey may be derived from Odin. We have Odinswell, now corrupted to Odwell, the narrow road leading to the Springs - Odinswell.

The spring water was at one time believed to have mystic properties in the cure of disease of the eye, and until the beginning of this century people came from far and near to take away large bottles of the water for some cure or other.

Although well dressing is not recorded it probably took place. It is, however, known that until the middle of last century an annual festival was held at the springs. Tables and chairs were set out with glasses and wine, and Ashwell and Baldock people made merry. History fails to record whether a toast was drunk to the nine sister spring, Odin's well or Mimer's fountain, but there was here unmistakeable evidence of an ancient custom being handed down, of our pagan ancestors following a feast or festival with an orgy of drinking on the banks of Odin's well.

'Ashwell Spring Head Watercress' was one of the cries of London in the last century.

In the 1920s, Gertie Bryant, Dr. Woodforde's maid, often collected a jug of the then pure water for the Doctor's table. Whilst in the 50s, I was told that the last wish of an old lady was a glass of water from the springs.

The Springs c.1900. Note Cottage and Cob Wall – all gone (Museum)

The Pestilence

That terrible pestilence, the Black Death, swept across Europe like a scourge from heaven. First of all, why Black Death? Well, it appears that in many cases the disease was recognised by dark blisters or swellings appearing on the skin of the victim; these were actually caused by small haemorrhages.

The plague which is said to have wiped out almost half the population of England, which at that time was estimated to be about 4 million, would seem to have struck Africa in 1345 and went on to Asia, Turkey and Greece. Records show that it had reached Italy by 1348. To give some idea of the magnitude of this terrible disease, of the 1,200,000 pilgrims who celebrated Easter in Rome that year only ten per cent survived, whilst over a period of five months Florence suffered 100,000 deaths.

As 1348 drew to a close the plague crossed the Channel, spreading rapidly. The Abbey of Westminster was badly hit. Symon de Byrchester, who was the patron of the Church of St. Mary the Virgin at Ashwell, perished, together with twenty-six of his monks. Hertfordshire is believed to have suffered greatly; the epidemic was at its height in April, and is said to have lingered on in the north of the county until late summer. At St. Albans Abbey, Abbot Mentmore and forty-seven monks died.

There is no record of the names of the victims who died at Ashwell or the numbers; as elsewhere the pestilence caused fear and panic. The town at that time was practically self-supporting, with something like half of the inhabitants dead or dying; for those who survived it was just that, a case of survival.

We know that the section of the churchyard next to Mill Street was used to bury the victims; it has been said that huge pits were dug and the corpses with or without shrouds were thrown in. Although most of the churchyard has been buried in, over and over again for about five centuries, this section has remained untouched, either in fear of unearthing once again the dread disease, or as a monument to those who died.

There is a permanent memorial; someone, only God knows who, carved it deeply in what have been described as Latin elegiacs, in old English letters with some curiously Greek characteristics, ten feet high on the clunch stone inner wall of the tower of Ashwell church. It is believed that the church, dedicated to St Mary the Virgin, was begun at the dawn of the fourteenth century on the site of an earlier church, the work being held up for several years due to the Black Death and not completed until 1381. There was in all probability still scaffolding inside the tower from which the carver worked, and carved these words: "1350. Pitiable, violent, savage, the dreadful plague. At the end the sinful folk survive to bear witness". The inscription can only be read in part. But high and low, monk and layman, were swept away and Ashwell was a very different place before and after 1350.

The Guild of St John the Baptist

On the south side of High Street, across the market square from the parish church of St. Mary the Virgin, the Bishop of Lincoln, the then Chancellor, and George, Duke of

Clarence, the brother of King Edward IV, the patrons, re-established the Guild of St. John the Baptist in 1476. It is one of the five guilds recorded in Hertfordshire.

William Freeman, a merchant of Ducklake, Ashwell, had left 6s. 8d. - one third of £1 - to the Guild in 1457.

The Guildhouse, an oaken-framed building with wattle-and-daub infilling and overhanging upper storey, is now divided into two dwelling houses and a baker's shop.

In the nineteenth century the heavily beamed interior was partitioned to form several shops with living accommodation, occupied by a baker, a tailor, a tinsmith and a carrier who undertook deliveries by a horse-drawn vehicle to neighbouring towns and villages.

During the fifteenth century, the Guild of St. John the Baptist became an important factor in the town and district. The endowments included arable land paying from 4d. to 1s. 4d. per acre, pasture on average being 2s. 10d. per acre. An annual rent of £1. 7s. 6d was paid to the Bishop of London. A stipulation of one of the payments was that a red rose was included. Another payment was 8d. for the purchase of two capons.

The parish church allowed the use of an altar, the guild providing the endowment for a priest, whose duties included mass said daily for the past and present brothers and sisters of the guild, and prayers for the king who had granted the licence.

William Sewster of Glitton, sometime a Mercer of London, left 3s 4d to the Fraternity of St. John the Baptist in 1505, while a document in the muniment room of Westminster Abbey states:

"Whereas King Henry VIII granted to the Abbot and Convent of Westminster his license to hold market at Ashwell, County Herts, on every Thursday throughout the year, and three fairs, on or about the transfiguration of Jesus Christ, St. Hugh Bishop, and St. Valentine Martyr, and a Pie Powder Court at all markets and fairs. Now therefore John (Iship) Abbat and Prior and Convent of Westminster, grant to William Sewster, William Lecheworth, Henry Bigrave and Richard Clerke, Wardens of the Fraternity or Gild of St. John the Baptist in the church of St. Mary at Ashwell, the fair and Pie Powder Court at St. Valentines feast. Dat in Chapter July 28 1523."

But the days of the Guild were numbered, for Henry VIII turned his avaricious eyes on Ashwell. His commission appointed on February 14, 1547, "for the survey of all Chantries, Gilds, Obits, Lights, etc., in the County of Hertford", recorded that John Sewster, of Glitton, Ashwell, contributed 9d. in 1547. John Sewster, of Steeple Morden, Cambridgeshire, trained in the law, a bencher of the Middle Temple, a commissioner of the peace in Hertfordshire, member of the commissions for jail delivery and sewers, attorney to the court of wards and liveries, and commissioner for levying the subsidy in Odsey hundred, Hertfordshire, was also among the gentlemen who in 1547 contributed towards the Guild of St. John the Baptist the sum of 2s.10½d.

The survey of 1547 also states: "Thomas Daye of thage of liiij yeres is Brotherhead Preste, a man of good behaviour and well lerned, exersyenge hymselfe in techinge of childerne".

The survey also records sixteen ounces of plate owned by the guild, ten of which were of parcel-gilt. When the Guild was suppressed its lands, property and plate were confiscated, but one small item was apparently overlooked by the king's commission, or perhaps smuggled away by the priest or a member of the guild, to be discovered nearly 400 years later in a farmhouse which was once the property of the guild, for in 1927 the owner of the farm placed on loan to the Ashwell museum a parcel-gilt silver reliquary. This small object, believed to be a beautiful example of the work of a fifteenth-century silversmith, bore on one side the sacred monogram I.H.S., and on the other side the lamb and flag of St. John the Baptist.

A member of an old Ashwell family of drapers, lawyers and divines, William Bill, in 1574 surrendered to Nicholas West a house situated in the High Street called le Guild house, or St John's house, or le Brotherhood house.

Adjoining the fifteenth-century guildhouse is a cottage, its front covered with plaster pargetry, bearing the date 1681. The County historians and Guide books describe this cottage as The Guildhouse, but its structure is of a later date than 1476, and the fact that it is built against the fifteenth-century timber-framed building, the gable end timbers of which can be clearly seen in the upper rooms of the cottage, proves beyond doubt that this could not have been The Guildhouse of St. John the Baptist.

** In 1478 the Duke of Clarence came to a sad end. It is recorded that he met his death in a butt of Malmsey wine.*

Nonconformists

John Bunyan preached in many towns and villages within twenty miles of Bedford and formed or gathered communities in them. It was his practice not to form converts in such places into separate churches but to affiliate them upon or incorporate them in his church at Bedford.

Bunyan applied for licences for meeting places in six counties for Protestant Dissenters under the Declaration of Indulgence 1672. Of the nineteen in Bedfordshire, one was for George Pridden's house at Edworth. The only one in Hertfordshire was for the house of Thos. Morrise in Ashwell.

At a church meeting held at Gamlingay on April 7th 1672 "Sister Mauris of Ashwell and Mary Prutton of Edworth were received into the fellowship". From notes made by the Rev. J.B. Millsom, pastor of the Independent chapel 1852-93 it is impossible to say whether any or if any, how much of Bunyan's work survived him, or whether at the end of the eighteenth century any part of it entered into the foundation of the Independent Church at Ashwell.

The rise of evangelical Noncomformity in Ashwell, as in many places, is connected with the great revival of the eighteenth century. Among the Calvinistic Methodists, John Berridge, Rector of Everton, Beds, stands forth very prominently. During the second half of the eighteenth century he was one of the most popular preachers in the area; people from miles around were in the habit of attending his services at Everton. He came to Ashwell and held a number of services in a barn at Westbury Farm, then owned by the Christy family. To quote Mr. Millsom "That his labour was successful there is no doubt". After some years, a place of meeting for a separate congregation was obtained, licensed and fitted out for worship. This building had been either a brewhouse or a malting standing in front of the present chapel and close to the street.

In or about 1793 a church was formed based on the principles held by "Independents" and Mr. Barfield, who was residing in Royston at the time, became the first minister, being publicly ordained then, as now, according to the custom, by prayer, charge and laying on of hands.

The congregation increased so much that it became necessary to build a larger place of worship. A new chapel was built and opened in April 1830. On the night of February 2nd 1850 a great fire broke out in Ashwell and destroyed a large part of the village, and with it the chapel. One circumstance in connection with the destruction of the chapel is so curious and yet so characteristic as to deserve record. A large sum of money was subscribed for those who had suffered. After all claims had been met a surplus of £400 remained in the hands of the vicar, the Rev. Henry Morice, and Mr. E.K. Fordham. The Independents thought this surplus or part of it should have been allotted towards rebuilding the chapel. But it was not. The £400 was given to Hitchin Infirmary and to this day one ward at the hospital is known as Ashwell ward. The people rebuilt the chapel and it was opened in 1852 when the Rev. J.B. Millsom accepted the call to Ashwell. His ministry covered the period of 41 years. In his farewell address he said his pastorate had not been without its disappointments and sorrows. He had keenly felt the migrations from his charge of the most vigorous and promising young folk to the larger towns, their number being equal to double the congregation he was leaving. At the Valedictory Meeting many Church of England friends were present.

Only two or three Sundays before the Rev. H.W. Hodgson, Rector of the parish, who came there three years before Mr. Millsom's arrival, had preached his farewell sermon, when Mr. Millsom and his congregation went in a body to the parish church.

The church remained without a Pastor for nearly twelve months until the Rev. C.C. Edwards of Batley entered upon the ministry on Sunday June 11th 1893. Individual Communion cups were introduced in 1909. The Rev. William Morgan was Pastor from 1910-1916. For the rest of the war years, services were conducted by lay preachers and students although a Rev. Hooper served for a short period.

The Rev. Arthur M. Perkins was Pastor from 1919 until his death in 1943. The next Pastor, the Rev. Herbert W. Hard, served the congregation from 1945-1949 and from 1949 to 1959 Mr. J. Griffiths served as Lay Pastor. After Mr. Griffiths left Ashwell, services were conducted by various lay preachers including Mr. F. Sillence, at that time Editor of the Royston Crow. Mr. Sillence was called to be Lay Pastor in September 1961. The Manse in Kingsland Way was sold in the late 1960s. The church, at that time Congregational, became United Reformed, by a majority, not a unanimous vote, in 1972. Mr. Fred Sillence celebrated 30 years as its Pastor in September 1991.

On the 14th of March 1692 the following application was sent to the Archdeacon of Huntingdon:

"We, part of the inhabitants of Ashwell doe desire you to register the house of Stephen Ingre of the same parish for a Meeting House, he liveth in the middle of the towne in Hye Streete. Witness our hands from Ashwell. Edward Waller. Senior. William Chapman. Robert Bacon. Thos. Gregorie. Stephen Ingre." On May 30th 1693 Thos. Mackeris. Edw. Waller. Wm. Chapman. Richard Bygrave and Stephen Ingre desired "to register the barn of Richard Bygrave, glazier for a meeting house in the midst of the towne aforesaid". In the next century the tone of the application was very different. "These are to certifie that a congregation of Protestant Dissenters doe intend to meet for religious worship at the house of Thos Mackaris in the parish of Ashwell. 11th Nov. 1708. Wm Bedford. Thos Mackaris. Wm. Mayes. Wm. Sharpe."

Ashwell's first Wesleyan chapel was built in Church Lane, probably in the 1850s or 60s. It became necessary to build a larger chapel, in High Street in 1880. The members included a school mistress, who was also the organist, Wilfred Bryant and Silas Worboys, the wheelwrights, with their families, a butcher, a baker, and a number of working class people. Whilst the hymn singing at the parish church was slow and deliberate, at the Wesleyans it was loud and went with a swing. A minister, as now, was responsible for a circuit of several chapels and one or more dedicated men in each area were known as local preachers, who conducted the morning or evening service at their own or other chapels in the circuit.

After the second world war, there was a decline in the number of worshippers at all churches, and as buildings aged, and the cost of repairs rose, so it became difficult to maintain the chapel, and in 1977 the members decided to amalgamate with the United Reformed Church. In 1979 the chapel was sold, pulled down, and the site used for houses.

My publisher, Norman Gurney, supplied me with notes on the Ashwell Strict Baptists and their chapel in Gardiners Lane, where he attended in his youth. For the use of the Baptist followers, Mr Flitton of Radwell Mill registered a cottage for services. James Martin, a harness maker, Septimus Sears and John Warburton all preached there. With increasing numbers attending, it was found necessary to build the pleasant little Strict Baptist chapel with its white painted scalloped barge boards and iron gates in Gardiners Lane, which was opened in 1854 by the three Ministers. On Christmas Day of that same year a mass baptismal service took place at Radwell Mill. The Minister, James Martin, baptised seven women and eight men, seven from Ashwell and eight from Walkern. The baptising in Radwell lake at the Mill head was followed by the Lord's Supper at which at least 30 people partook. To end this great Christmas day Mr Flitton, the master of the Mill, invited all those present to a good dinner of boiled round of beef and leg of mutton, followed by plum pudding. It was during the 1920s that the chapel in Gardiners Lane became known as Zoar Strict Baptist Chapel.

A gate in Swan Street led to the little Co-op hall, a building originally built late in the 19th Century as the club room of the Stag Public House Sick Benefit Club. When in the 1920s the Co-operative Society bought the pub, the club room at the rear was let out for small private functions, social evenings, etc. It was here that a little group of people, including Cowman George Noble, Milkman Arthur Lambert and others, known as the Brethren, met regularly to hold religious services. I believe the services or meetings were less formal than those of the other religious bodies and attracted quite a number of village children. In the 1960s these services discontinued.

During the eighteenth century the Quakers, or Friends as they became known, were active in Ashwell, with their own Meeting House. However, this timber framed building in Back Street was destroyed in the Great Fire of Ashwell of 1850; the roof tiles were salvaged and re-used on the roof of Westrope's shop. If you take the footpath, known as Quakers Walk, off Silver Street, as you climb over the stile and look to the left you will see the Quakers' burial ground, the neat headstones rather overgrown and hemmed in by the modern houses of "Angell's Meadow". It would appear that thereafter Ashwell's Quakers met at Royston or elsewhere.

Doves and Gunpowder

Dovehouses were of national importance in the seventeenth century in the production of gunpowder.

J.E. Cussans, in his History of Hertfordshire, published in 1873, states: "The manufacture of saltpetre was formerly carried on to a great extent in Ashwell and neighbourhood.

About the year 1640, John Morton of Ashwell, who had been "a workman in the misterie of making saltpeeter 28 yeares," presented a petition to the king's commissioners praying for the exclusive right to manufacture saltpetre in Ashwell.

In another communication he details abuses of which Edward Thornhill, the then Deputy Commissioner for the counties of Hertford, Bedford, Buckingham and Northampton, had been guilty.

Morton says "Hee concealeth dove-howses wherein the mine of saltpetre is utterly decaied, and spareth other dove-houses which are good to work upon, whereby the service is much hindered, dovehowses being the principall nourceries of saltpetre".

From R. Chamber's Book of Days, published in 1866, we learn that a patent was granted in 1625 to Sir John Brook and Thomas Russel for obtaining saltpetre, for the manufacture of gunpowder, from animal excrement, from the soil of slaughter-houses and stables, and even from the floors of dwelling houses; but it appears that the patent did not immediately produce a supply equal to the demand, for in the year 1627, the third year of the reign of Charles I, a proclamation was issued to remedy the inconvenience arising to the service from the want of a full and proper supply of nitre for the gunpowder manufacturers.

It first set forth that the saltpetre makers were never able to furnish the realm with a third part of the saltpetre required, more especially in time of war, and then proceeded to state that since a patent had been granted to Sir John Brook and Thomas Russel for the making of saltpetre by a new invention they were authorised to collect the animal fluids (which were ordered by this same proclamation to be preserved by families for this purpose) from house to house once in twenty-four hours in summer and once in forty-eight hours in winter.

This proclamation was offensive and highly inconvenient to the people, and the frequent visits of the saltpetre man and his agents would be anything but welcome.

This, however, was not the worst. All soils throughout the kingdom which were impregnated with animal matter were claimed by the Crown for this peculiar purpose, and the same proclamation empowered the saltpetre makers to dig up the floors of all dovehouses, stables, cellars, slaughterhouses, etc., for the purpose of carrying away the earth, and prohibited the proprietors from relaying such floors with anything but mellow earth, to afford greater facilities to the digger. An obvious consequence was that individuals anxious to preserve their premises from injury from this ruinous digging resorted to bribery.

The proclamation of 1627 ordered municipal bodies to maintain, at their own expense, works for the manufacture of saltpetre from the refuse of their localities. In 1633 an order was made by the corporation of Nottingham to the effect that no person without leave from the mayor and common council should remove any soil, except to places appointed for the reception of such matter, nor should any such matter be sold to any foreigner (stranger) without their licence, and in 1637 William Burrows agreed to be made a burgess of Nottingham on condition of freeing the town of all charges relating to the saltpetre works.

Even in 1589 the people of Newark appealed to Lord Burghley, the "Lord Highe Threasurer of Englande", that there was a general complaint by the whole country against John Ffox, saltpetre maker. These vexatious and mischievous visits were put a stop to in 1656 by the passing of an Act forbidding saltpetre makers to dig in houses and enclosed lands without leave of the owners.

After the discovery and importation of rough nitre from the East Indies the practice of obtaining it by the process fell into gradual disuse, and thus the country was relieved of one of the greatest annoyances to which it had ever been subject.

Today only one of the 17th Century dovehouses remains in Ashwell, the Dixies Farm dovehouse, of red brick with a tiled roof, probably built at the time when John Morton was the "saltpetre king" of Ashwell. The inner walls of the dovehouse are honeycombed with hundreds of square nesting holes.

There are still people who remember a large dovehouse in the rectory grounds, circular in shape and with a thatched roof. Just off the High Street at Whitby Farm a huge dovehouse was destroyed during the great fire in 1850, while Dove Cottages, near the springs, record the site of a dovehouse, the subject of a watercolour by one of the Lucas family of Hitchin. The Grange Dovehouse, in Elbrook Lane, still retains its outer shape but its interior has been changed for human habitation.

Railroad Navvies and the Great Fire of 1850

During the twentieth century we have seen giant earth-moving machines dig their way through the countryside, tremendous quantities of steel, concrete and tarmac used in the building of bridges, flyovers and roads to form our motorway system.

We are inclined to forget that, perhaps an even bigger operation took place during the last two-thirds of the nineteenth century, without machines. By the year 1900, hundreds of thousands of tons of soil and rock had been moved by wheelbarrow, shovel, pickaxe, explosive and the hard labour of thousands of navvies, working twelve hours a day, to build something like 20,000 miles of railway.

The branch line from Hitchin to Royston was built by an independent local concern, the Royston and Hitchin Railway, and opened on October 21st 1851. In 1923 it became part of the London & North Eastern Railway.

A large gang of navvies and their women folk were living in a little shanty town, complete with its own pub named "The Hit and Miss" at Slip End, half-way between Baldock and Odsey. (With wages of eighteen shillings a week, twice that of the farm worker, they could afford to buy their beer by the gallon.)

At eleven o'clock on Saturday night February 2nd, 1850, a farm worker started a fire which destroyed much of Ashwell. It was reported that the flames were seen in

Reproduction from a Booklet published about the Fire shortly afterwards, the sketch being by Miss Charlotte Morice (Museum)

Luton, and one correspondent with a vivid imagination, stated that the flames lit up the night sky so brilliantly that one could see to read a newspaper in the streets of Buntingford.

So it is not surprising that the navvies at Slip End saw the light, and came down into Ashwell where the Vicar, the Rev. Henry Morice, had organised a chain of buckets to throw water on the flames in an attempt to check the fire until the arrival of the two great fire engines from Hitchin.

In the extreme heat of the burning thatch and timber, one of the railway navvies poured a bucket of water over the vicar, after which he was laid low with pneumonia, and at a meeting later in the year, the vestry clerk announced that the worthy vicar had died.

The clerk went on to record: "The question, respecting the rateable value of the railway through this parish was considered but the matter was deferred for the present". In 1854 it was ordered that the overseers should employ Mr. Thurnall, solicitor of Royston, to defend the parish, in conjunction with the other parishes on the line. It was not until 1859 that "the vestry clerk having stated the offer made by the Eastern Railway Company to have the railway now in their occupation in this parish rated at a rental of £50 per annum, the company paying all arrears calculated on the said sum of £50. It was proposed by Mr. John Sale, seconded by Mr. E. Bacon, that the said railway be rated at £50."

A serious accident in 1866 brought the branch line into the news. Mr. C.F. Harper, a Therfield grocer, an eye-witness of the occurrence, said that the 9.50 am train from Hitchin to Cambridge had left Ashwell and Morden station, and was proceeding towards Royston when, within a hundred yards of the Litlington level crossing, the engine suddenly left the rails, ran round in a circle and became embedded in a field of barley. Both driver Hunt and fireman Clark were killed. The engine was later taken to Hitchin station yard, where it was photographed by Mr. T.B. Latchmore, the well-known Hitchin photographer. An inquiry into the accident found that the privately owned section of the railway had not been properly maintained, with the result that the company was obliged to sell out to the Great Northern Railway Company. Mr. Michael Horsfield, of Clevedon, near Bristol, tells me that his grandfather George Horsfield was stationmaster at Ashwell from about 1865-1869. During the year 1869 Mary Ann, the wife of George, expressed a wish to visit a London consultant about her forthcoming fourth child; George agreed and suggested suitable times of trains.

As Mary Ann entered the carriage, George, on the spur of the moment, decided to accompany his wife. Alas, on their return to Ashwell station, George was informed that he was dismissed for leaving his post. The family moved to Hitchin, where later that year Fred was born, to be followed by eleven more children. The former stationmaster, not wishing to sever his connection with the railways completely, became an insurance broker, dealing with passenger insurance.

For many years Ashwell had a very busy goods yard, serving not only Ashwell, but the two Mordens and the other villages around. Herbert Fordham of Odsey and Abraham Christy of Ashwell both had coal depots here; best Staveley coal retailed at one shilling per hundredweight in 1860. The railway carried beers from Fordham's Ashwell brewery to London and Yarmouth, fertilisers from the Odsey coprolite mill, hay for London's horses, and livestock to wherever livestock was needed, and coming in were huge "pockets" of Kent hops for the two Ashwell breweries, sacks of sugar and rice, salt in half hundredweight blocks, and all the necessary supplies for the grocers, saddlers, shoemakers, tinkers and tailors, delivered daily by a horse-drawn wagon.

Today, all those supplies come to the villages by road, and the goods yard is, guess what? A depot for those earth-moving machines.

The Coproliters

The trailer and lorry loads of plastic bags containing artificial fertilisers are a familiar sight in the countryside. To the farmer today artificials are as essential as the mechanisation of his farm, but his father will remember the days of horse-drawn implements, farmyard manure, and a few sacks of artificials to be used very sparingly.

North Hertfordshire was one of the first sources of artificials. In 1845, John (later Sir John) Lawes, one of the founders of the Rothamsted Agricultural Research Station, discovered by experiment the value of superphosphate as a fertiliser. It was found to be especially good for turnips.

The raw materials, known as coprolites (pronounced "copperlites" by the diggers), were to be found in a belt of country, from two to six miles wide and fifty miles long, stretching from Harlington in Bedfordshire to Soham in Cambridgeshire, and passing through Hinxworth and Ashwell in Hertfordshire.

Coprolites, petrified droppings of pre-historic animals, together with corals, sea urchins, ammonites, fish, reptiles and birds, were found in a layer six to twelve inches deep in the lower greensand, between nine and twenty-five feet below the surface.

Several companies were engaged in the digging of coprolites between the years 1860 and 1880. They paid a royalty of from £60 to £150 per acre for the rights, with the condition that the topsoil be carefully removed and later, after removal of the coprolites and the backfilling of the marl and subsoil, replaced, rendering the land fit for cultivation again within two or three years.

At a meeting of the Ashwell vestry held on March 25th, 1875, it was proposed by Mr. Tyndale and seconded by the Rev. J.B. Millson that the trustees of the Ashwell charities be empowered to treat with Mr. Lawes for the purchase of the coprolites in the land appertaining thereto.

The method of extracting the coprolites from the greensand was, of course, entirely by hand. A vertical trench was dug until the layer was reached, then worked in two or three stages according to the depth necessary.

The coprolites were then dug out, to be washed in a mill, a circular-rake type of machine driven by horse-power, water being poured in from high wooden aqueducts. This need of water led to the sinking of wells, unless the excavations were near a river.

It was estimated that 100 cubic yards of earth had to be removed to gain one ton of phosphate.

The cost of removal, cartage, plant and supervision amounted to fourpence or fivepence per cubic yard. The diggers received from threehalfpence to threepence per cubic yard.

According to notes made by the late Henry Bowman, a good digger could earn from thirty shillings to two pounds per week, while an agricultural worker was paid ten shillings per week. Then, as men left the farms to join the coproliters, farm wages were raised to twenty shillings. In some areas whole farms lay derelict for several years due to the shortage of labour.

The Ashwell census figures are interesting: 715 persons in 1801, 1235 in 1841, 1425 in 1861, 1507 in 1871, 1576 in 1881. Health improvements may have had a lot to do with the rise in population.

As the population increased so did the number of public-houses, from three in 1831 to twenty-four in 1881. Four of these were opened up in the coprolite area especially for the thirsty diggers: the Tumble Down Dick, now Bluegates farmhouse; the Labour in Vain, now a small farmhouse at Northfields; the Cuckoo, now a house half-way between Ashwell and Hinxworth; and the New Found Out, a cottage in Bennetts Lane, this last one referring to coprolites. At Guilden Morden a public house appropriately named the Diggings was in use until a few years ago.

To supply these and many other inns and hotels, Messrs. Edward King Fordham and Oswald Fordham set up their brewery in Mill Street, and Messrs. John Sale and Benjamin Christy started another in the west end.

The public-houses were open all day long, and the skittle alley at the Bushel and Strike was in constant use. One local character took a twenty-pint wooden bottle of beer to work daily.

There were many tough customers in the gangs, and fights and brawls frequently occurred. Great excitement was aroused when an earthenware vessel was found containing a large number of silver coins bearing raised designs, some in the form of stars. At Odsey, near Ashwell station, there is still a building known as the mill room. The coprolites from Hinxworth and Ashwell were taken to this mill to be ground into a fine powder, then treated with sulphuric acid, thus producing superphosphate of lime. There were other mills at Meldreth and Royston stations.

It was estimated that the maximum yield of coprolites in England was 55,000 tons a year. The importation of cheaper supplies from Scandinavia, Florida, Algeria and

Tunis, together with the exhaustion of the coprolite beds, saw the end of the industry. By 1901 Ashwell's population had dropped to 1,281.

Foreign Fields

The great war with Napoleon ended leaving Britain exhausted, with heavy taxation, a debt of £800 million, and general distress. A series of bad harvests caused great unemployment and distress in our agricultural areas.

At Ashwell, the worthy vicar together with the churchwardens and overseers of the poor, enlisted the aid of all employers of labour. Consequently, at a Vestry meeting held on November 7th, 1832, "It was agreed that each of the undersigned will take and employ one settled inhabitant of the Parish for every forty acres which he shall occupy within the said Parish, and that he will not employ any boy not belonging to the Town, while any belonging to the Parish is unemployed. Henry Morice, Vicar; Wm. Thompson, Churchwarden; Saml. Bowman, Wm. Kirbyshire, Overseers; John Sale, Thos. Chapman, Jo. Kirbyshire, Benj. Christy, Wm. Bacon, J. Lees, Rd. Westrope." A Vestry meeting held on June 1st, 1835 "Ordered that a portion of the surplus labourers be employed at the Quarries to dig stones".

The following year brought new hope to a number of the unemployed and a great adventure to new lands. At a Vestry meeting on May 12th, 1836 it was decided "That the sum of sixty pounds be forthwith raised by the churchwardens and overseers as a fund or contribution for defraying the expense of the emigration of Poor Persons having settlements in this Parish and being willing to emigrate, to be paid out of the rates raised".

Again in April 1854 "The Vestry resolved that the sum of Fifteen Pounds be forthwith raised for Poor Persons to emigrate". The Ashwell Vestry records do not give the names of any of those emigrants, but the museum owns a complete set of emigration documents, including "Directions to be observed by persons wanting Free Passage to Queensland"; a "List of Necessary Articles for ship use for Free Passengers"; and the "Free Passage Certificate by the Black Ball Line to Queensland" bearing the name of Arthur Edwards.

On October 20th, 1865 Arthur Edwards went aboard the 1500-ton "Golden City", having said farewell to his relatives and friends at Ashwell. The directions, issued by the Queensland Government Emigration Offices of Old Broad Street, London, stated that to be eligible for a free single passage, a man must be either a farm labourer, vine dresser, gardener, roadmaker, miner, quarryman, blacksmith, bricklayer, mason, sawyer, carpenter, wheelwright or shipbuilder.

Of clothing, males must take not less than six shirts, six pairs of stockings, two warm flannel or Guernsey shirts, two pairs of strong shoes and two complete suits of external clothing. A female's clothing had to consist of six shifts, two warm flannel petticoats, six pairs of stockings, two pairs of strong shoes, two strong gowns, one of which must be warm. These articles were to be taken together with the necessary brushes and combs and clothes brushes for cleanliness.

It was advised to have not less than the above outfit, but the larger the stock of clothing the better for health and comfort during the voyage, which usually lasted about four months, and as the voyagers had to pass through very hot and very cold weather, they had to be prepared for both.

The whole quantity of baggage for each adult was not to exceed half a ton. Feather beds were especially prohibited. On arrival in the colony, free passengers were at perfect liberty to engage themselves to anyone willing to employ them and to make their own bargain for wages.

Once aboard the "Golden City", Arthur was issued with a bed and a pair of sheets, a water bottle, washbasin, a pint drinking mug, knife, fork, two spoons and $3^{1}/_{2}$lb of marine soap. According to the contract ticket, each adult would receive three quarts of water daily, exclusive of what is necessary for cooking, and a weekly allowance of 3 lb. of bread or biscuit, not inferior in quality to navy biscuit, 2 lb. wheaten flour, 1 lb. oatmeal, $^{1}/_{2}$lb. rice, $1^{1}/_{2}$ lb. peas, 2 lb. potatoes, $1^{1}/_{4}$ lb. beef, 1 lb. pork, 2 oz. tea, 1 lb. sugar, 2 oz. salt, $^{1}/_{2}$ oz. mustard, $^{1}/_{4}$ oz. butter.

Extensive gold fields in Australia had been discovered in May 1851, although the news had reached England only in September of that year. According to a report of the day, some little time elapsed before the news became sufficiently assured to tell upon the public mind. Its effects, however, were soon to show.

During the first four months of 1852, the number of emigrants to Australia doubled. Arthur Edwards was one of the emigrants in 1865, but whether he joined the gold diggers or worked on the land no one seems to know. However, substantial evidence remains in Ashwell of one emigrant gold digger.

Still remembered by some of the older residents, William Pack Edwards left Ashwell in the 1870s, and after only a few years in the Australian gold fields, returned a wealthy man. In the High Street, Bill Edwards built a house, typical of the Victorian period, with two bay windows for the display of aspidistras. A stone tablet above the porch bears the date 1881 and the name The Adelong. Below this, carved on the ornamental keystone are an emu and a kangaroo.

The former gold digger moved into the new house with his sister Jane Pack Edwards and a maid. In the dining room, a white cockatoo stood or sat on its perch for fifty years, while proudly displayed in the drawing room was a glass case containing mementos of Australia, emus' eggs, the tail feathers of a lyre bird, a tiny pair of embroidered Chinese shoes, samples of rocks and minerals, quartz, silver and copper ore, stream tin, antimony, coal and asbestos.

A polished grey stone in the United Reformed Churchyard records the fact that William Pack Edwards died in 1911 aged seventy-four and Jane Pack Edwards died in 1935.

Ashwell Show at Elbrook

For as long as I can remember August Bank Holiday has been Show Day at Ashwell. Of course there have been variations, flower and vegetable, veteran car rallies and dog shows, but the horse has always had a place in the Ashwell Show.

Even when the tractor took the place of the horse, we still had the Cambridgeshire fox hounds led into the ring by a horseman, and there was a man with a dancing horse. For some years now the horse has made its way back into the show and plays a very important part in it. Several thousand people come to Elbrook meadow on this Bank Holiday, and at some time during the day some of the visitors must look up at Elbrook House with its many chimneys and steep tiled roofs and ponder on its past and the people who have lived there.

The late Henry Bowman wrote "Helbeck is identified with Elbrook, beck is of Danish origin and may suggest that the Danes lived here". No one seems sure exactly when Elbrook House was built.

Oswald, the second son of Edward George Fordham, of Odsey Grange, was born in 1819 and a stone slab in Ashwell churchyard records his early death: "Oswald Fordham. Esq. Died July 21st, 1863. A Justice of the Peace for this County. The high intellectual qualities of his mind united to the kindest heart and most noble generosity of soul inspired universal respect and affection". At the age of 18 Oswald Fordham bought Ashwell Brewery from his father for £100, and at some time during his short life he built the main part of Elbrook House. He also fell in love. (More of that later).

He left Elbrook in trust to his nephew Edward Snow Fordham (then aged five) the first-born son of Edward King Fordham of Ashwell Bury.

Snow Fordham, as he was known locally, was a big man and the floor of his Napier motor car was specially strengthened to take his weight. Abrams, the chauffeur, wore a peaked cap with green livery, its buttons embossed with a peacock, the Fordham crest. Elbrook House was enlarged to provide nursery accommodation; friends and relatives from miles around came to gaze at the first bathroom in the area. The white enamelled bath shaped from sheet copper stood on a dais or platform in the centre of the room; prints of semi-nude classical Greek statues hung on the walls.

The family had three sons and two daughters. After public school and university Edward King, Oswald and Hugh all did the Continental tour accompanied by a tutor. The two oldest sons then went into the theatre, without the approval of the family, so they dare not use the family name. Hugh joined the staff of a bank in Paris and later became the foreign representative of a well known firm of perfumiers.

Edward Snow Fordham died in 1919. Annie, his widow, lived on at Elbrook House and died in 1931. I remember this very well because Fred Bray and I made the necessary arrangements for the interment in the Fordham vault in Ashwell churchyard.

There was an air of mystery about it all; Oswald the second son arrived to supervise the opening of the vault, (Edward King had died in 1922). He had a plan showing the positions of the various members of the family already in the vault and, as we removed the brick filling from the entrance, he told us the story of Oswald the first, an honourable and much respected young man who had hoped to carry on the Fordham name at Elbrook and the Fordham Brewery just over the river.

He had been very much in love until one day without warning he was jilted by his fiancee. He died aged 44 unmarried. The lady came to the funeral in 1863 and placed a package on the coffin as it was being lowered to the floor of the vault next to that of his mother. Ever since that day the Fordham family have been curious as to the contents of the package. The mystery has never been solved.

When we opened the vault only one coffin was intact, two lead shells remained but their outer coffins had disappeared, as had the other three in the vault. Somewhere underneath a heap of decaying oak boards and bones the package still remains.

The death of Mrs Snow Fordham was certainly the end of an era. On the morning of the funeral Gilbert, the gardener, assisted by Abrams reverently lined the walls and floor of the shallow grave and screened the entrance to the vault with barrow loads of ivy, moss and spring flowers. It was a sad day for both; they knew the house was to be sold. For Abrams, apart from helping to line the grave, it was a busy day. He was up early to polish the old Napier and "brasso" the bonnet and headlamps and then fetch several loads of mourners.

The Rev Henry A. Griffith, the rector, conducted the service knowing that it was the end of afternoon tea, home made buttered scones and seed cake with tea poured by one of the maids, among the little glass-topped tables filled with silver and china knick knacks in the drawing room at Elbrook.

After the mourners had left the churchyard, we carefully eased the coffin on to the iron bearers and sealed the vault. Although it was only intended for seven coffins we had been asked to make it possible, when the time came, for Oswald the second son to rest beside his mother.

Before the contents of the house were sold I was asked to help sort out some of the personal effects of Edward Snow Fordham which had remained untouched since his death in 1919. One drawer in a large filing cabinet was filled with intimate details of cases dealt with at Dalston Magistrates Court, another contained correspondence, estate accounts and several sealed envelopes which we found contained a daguerreotype photograph on glass of Edward Snow as a boy, a third century coin of Carthage, a 16th century floor tile found in Ashwell church in 1868 and a metal figure with blue enamel eyes, from a 13th century Limoges shrine. These, together with a photograph of Edward King Fordham of Ashwell Bury in his uniform as High Sheriff of Bedfordshire and his sword of office were presented by the family to Ashwell Museum.

The house and grounds were sold to Mrs Phyllis Fordham and remained in the Fordham family for another 32 years. Some modernisation took place which included the removal of the ancient bath and its dais; the prints of semi-nudes went in the sale of contents. The new occupants, Colonel Eustace and Mrs Barbara Hill (a sister of Mrs Phyllis Fordham) with their children Anthony, Julian, Cynthia and Robin, settled in and life at Ashwell went on as before. Charles Reynold's sweet peas and runner beans still gained first prizes at the annual flower show in the meadow, the pleasant aroma of malt still drifted over the village and lorry loads of Fordham's ales went out to quench the thirst of folks in at least four counties until World War Two when Hitler took a hand in the story of Elbrook House.

With their two sons in the Royal Air Force and the two daughters married, and the problems of rationing, the difficulties of heating and running a house of this size forced the Hills to move into Redlands Grange and there were rumours in the village, which proved to be true, that Elbrook House was to be turned into flats.

The main block was let to Charles Christy, a London antique dealer; the hall doorway was sealed and the rear section was converted into Elbrook Flats. It remained like this until 1964 when the property was sold to a private buyer and once again became Elbrook House.

Oswald, the second son of Snow Fordham, died in the 1960s. His ashes were buried at Ashwell cemetery; he had either forgotten to make his wishes known, or his executors ignored them. So there is still one vacant space in the Fordham vault.

The present owners of Elbrook House are Dr Erasmus Barlow and his wife, Brigit. In 1990 her autobiographical book "A family affair" was published, dealing with her acceptance into the famous Darwin family when she married Erasmus, grandson of the famous scientist.

Ashwell Ghosts

It was about the year 1921 when I heard of the West End ghost; this mysterious figure, completely covered by a white shroud, had been seen perched on the high wall surrounding Mr. Joshua Page's brewery house and on dark nights it had the nasty habit of swooping hawklike down on to the road when one or more women or girls came past, but strangely was never seen by men or boys.

Years later I was shown a faded press cutting, dated 1911, "To the Editor, Herts & Cambs Reporter:

"Sir - Following up on the thread of Mr. W.B. Gerish's interesting article, my thoughts travel back to childhood days at Ashwell, and a story related to me by my mother. It would be during the lengthy ministry of Mr Morice, a former vicar of Ashwell. My mother was then the leading treble singer in the mixed choir at church and, as was her usual custom on Friday evenings in attending choir practice, she crossed the churchyard from the corner gate opposite the Merchant Taylors School and, as she was making her way to the chancel door, there seemed to be someone walking in the opposite direction from the vicarage to the same door.

"The moon was shining very brightly at the time; as my mother turned to enter the church, this figure, dressed in black and headless, glided noiselessly up to the door and without speaking vanished suddenly. My mother, overcome with this spectral disappearance, as she opened the chancel door fell unconscious on to the floor; the already assembled choir came to her aid and the practice was closed down for the evening.

"My mother was led to her home nearby. The shock having passed she was in future accompanied by some members of the choir on dark and windy nights for the choir practice, but to the end of her days this happening was always a real thing to her. Yours truly, A.C. Waldock."

Eventually I met Arthur Waldock, a very tall man, so tall in fact that in his youth he had been nicknamed "Willow tree". Like many village boys Arthur went to London to find work, settled in Dulwich and became a buyer for a firm of wholesale fruiterers at Spitalfields market. I learned that Georgina Covington was the maiden name of Arthur's mother and at the time of this occurrence she lived in the house now known as Ashe Cottage in Mill Street, and as the Rev. Henry Morice died in 1850 it must have happened before that year.

A well-known researcher into these mysteries came up with the following theory: the date about 1850 is, of course, most significant in the history of Ashwell. In the fourteenth century, the time of the Black Death and the fearful epidemic which struck the town, someone dragged himself to the church and carved a record of the catastrophe on the north wall of the tower. Could one of the soon-to-perish victims have carved the inscription as a final act? Halfway through the nineteenth century would be the 500th anniversary of this event.

It would be interesting to know whether anything was seen in the churchyard about that time this century. If not, perhaps no one of the required "sensitivity" to see such things was at the right place at the right time. If the spectre was indeed the carver of the inscription this would narrow the search considerably - so few had the required learning or the motive to put forth the effort to record a happening. A good guess would be the cleric in charge of Ashwell church - that is if the historical clues have been read correctly.

Certain late night travellers between Bygrave and Ashwell say they have seen a phantom coach drawn by two horses. This might be accounted for as follows. On the night of Sunday, November 26th 1871, Mr. and Mrs John Westrope, who had been to a dinner party at Weston, were safely returned to Prospect House, their home in Ashwell. However, on his way back to the Rose and Crown stables at Baldock, the hired coachman came to grief.

In a letter to Hertfordshire Notes and Queries, the late Reginald L. Hine wrote: "One wild night about thirty winters ago the driver of one of the Rose and Crown flies from Baldock was thrown into the stream by the culvert on the Bygrave road. My father found his body the next morning down stream." (The accident occurred at Cat Ditch, the origins of which Mr. Hine also explains as having "its rise in the parish of Sandon and, as it rushes down the Sandon hill in winter, may well be termed a waterfall. The average from bank to bank is about ten feet, this is just the sort of distance a well conditioned cat would spring at with confidence and clear ..." though there was no actual tradition of any cat having made the attempt. He adds that "in the summer months the stream is so diminished that a cat can walk through on dry feet".)

In his book of Ashwell notes, A.C. Waldock wrote: "I well remember the sad happening. My father and Fred Bryant were thrashing wheat at Bygrave: they passed the culvert about 4.30 am and heard nothing, it was pitch dark. About 8 am the sad news was brought to them; they shut down steam and went to see what had happened. The coachman had fallen off his seat and the swift current carried his body as far as Newnham Bottom culvert where Mr. Neville Hine found the body. The pair of carriage horses were lying in the water in the Bygrave Lane culvert, one dead, the other much injured. On the following Sunday solemn mention was made in the pulpits at Ashwell".

Poor Boy Made Good

Most of our towns, and many villages, boast a row of almshouses built especially for the use of aged local people or widows. Usually these houses were built, or at least paid for, by a wealthy local citizen, as for instance the almshouses at Hitchin and those in Baldock's wide main street.

At Ashwell a narrow lane bearing the name-plate Alms Lane connects the High

Street with Swan Street. At one end stood the Technical School built by Rupert Fordham in the 1890s in order to continue the education, through evening classes, of those boys who left school at the age of 12. The space between the "Technical" (as it was known) and a workshop was filled with two dilapidated houses which had originally been almshouses.

According to the churchwardens' account books there were almshouses at Ashwell in the 17th century. Whether they were built by a local benefactor or by the church is not recorded. They were not endowed and are not mentioned among the parish charities. The almshouses were the responsibility, and often the headache, of the churchwardens and overseers of the poor.

Towards the end of the nineteenth century, the new parish and rural district councils had taken over most of the duties of churchwardens, constables and overseers; it was probably at this time that the almshouses were sold. Benjamin Christy of Westbury Farm became the owner of the two in Alms Lane.

One of the dilapidated almshouses referred to earlier was occupied by an elderly brother and sister known as Jack Snack and Sally Mumfort - everyone seemed to have a nickname in those days. When Jack Snack died in the early 1920s, grief stricken Sally placed a bunch of flowers on his grave. The piece of card said quite simply "Gone but forgotten". Poor old Sally died soon after her brother. The cottages were condemned by the housing authority and the tenants of the second almshouse moved into one of the twenty-six council houses built on Station road.

In Hodwell (sometimes pronounced "Oddle") - the short road off High Street opposite the United Reformed Church - there stands today a block of six red brick almshouses. Built into the far end front corner is a stone which states "This Stone Was Laid By George Moss Esq July 4th 1904. H.W. BOWMAN Clerk to the P.C. C.W. HORSER Architect. F.J. BAILEY Builder".

I have a special interest in that stone. George Moss may have spread the mortar under the stone, maybe with an inscribed silver plated trowel, but it was my grandfather, John Sheldrick, who, with Peter Skerman, actually lowered the stone into position, after checking that the fingers of George were clear.

It is sixty years since I first enquired how George Moss, a poor village boy, found the money to build and endow the six Moss Cottage Homes, and even now there are a few questions unanswered. The Ashwell story was that George went up to London and ran a coffee stall at a railway station. His agreement stated that every train must stop at the coffee stall. Later when the company introduced express trains, George was paid substantial compensation.

When I was appointed a trustee of the Homes in 1948 I hoped to solve the mystery. However I gave up the search until fairly recently when by one of those unexpected strokes of luck Geoffrey Moss, a great-grandson of George, turned up on my doorstep, wishing to delve into his family history. After much exchange of information and, with the help of David Short of Ashwell Further Education Centre, Geoffrey himself carried on the search with the following results: John Moss, described in the records as a labourer/ publican, was born in 1790 and married Frances Harradine at Ashwell in 1822. They had six sons and one daughter.

The family, in 1841, were living in a house which stood in front of Dixies Cottage, 90 High Street. I remember the house well, because in 1920 my parents moved into

Dixies Cottage. The old house was demolished and the site became our front garden.

An interesting extract from the Court minutes of the Merchant Taylors Company of London, dated 25th October 1851 reads: "A letter from John Thomas, Headmaster of the Ashwell Merchant Taylors' School, told of the success in life of George Moss, a poor labourer's son, who was educated at the said school and had since by his persevering industry been enabled to support his parents, establish his brother in business and secure an independence for himself, and which he attributed solely to the education he received at the company's school".

In 1851 George, then only 28 years old, was licensee of a pub at Aldgate. In 1871 he turns up at the Gloucester Arms, Upper Place, Marylebone. Geoffrey Moss discovered that George either owned or managed public houses at Battersea, Camberwell and even as far away as Hastings.

George Moss seems to have made a major investment when, at 52 years of age, he bought the lease of a hotel at the Wiltshire town of Swindon - the town with its huge railway workshops, the home of the Great Western Railway, known in its day as "God's Wonderful Railway".

When Swindon station was built it included, as did a number of stations, a hotel over the station. Built into their contract, Rigbys the builders included a concession which gave them the legal rights to run this hotel, with a proviso that all trains, except royal trains, must pull up at the station for a ten minute break. Eventually Rigbys sold the lease and on April 7th 1875 it was purchased by George Moss for £45,000.

No one as yet can explain why, on 4th August 1880, George sold the lease for £35,000, thereby losing £10,000 - or could this be the clue I have been seeking all these years, the connection with that old Ashwell rumour, the proviso that all trains stop at George's coffee stall - some coffee stall! -the coming of express trains, and the compensation received?

Eventually, having made a fortune he retired and settled down at Upper Norwood, Surrey. Looking back at his early days in Ashwell he gave much thought to the struggles of the poorer people there and decided to share his good fortune with them. To this end he approached Henry Bowman, who among other things was clerk to Ashwell Parish Council.

In 1904 the six Moss Cottage Homes were built. The six homes are registered with the Charity Commissioners and the rules drawn up by George and his solicitor in 1905 state that the charity shall be managed by 13 trustees: The rector and churchwardens for the time being of Ashwell, four representative trustees and six co-optative trustees.

Rule 39 stated: "If any inmate shall be guilty of insobriety, insubordination, breach of regulations, or immoral or unbecoming conduct, they may be removed or have the stipend suspended". (The residents until about 1950 were paid five shillings a week in winter and four shillings in summer.)

The endowment of £2,000 was in three percent Debenture stock of the London and North Western railway company.

Ashwell Museum has several photographs celebrating the building of the homes: one of George Moss, complete with top hat, laying the foundation stone; another a group of people who attended the ceremony and a third of the benefactor himself bearing his signature. Henry Bowman was the unofficial clerk of the works and reported progress by postcard, postage one (old) penny, which George received the next day. Peter Greener, the curator of Ashwell Museum, is a collector of local viewcards and has acquired several of Henry's cards, some of which are included in this book.

Here I quote the eloquent words of the rector of Ashwell, the Rev. S.W.P. Webb, from the parish magazine of December 1904: "The poor of Ashwell have again been favoured this Christmastide, and good will and kindly thought for the aged poor and the necessitous was much in evidence. It was a pleasant sight to see so many well known ladies on charitable thoughts intent carrying full freighted goody baskets. It was not expected when the munificent gift of the Moss Cottage Homes was completed and vested in the hands of trustees that the benefactions of former years would be continued but the donor, Mr. G. Moss, feared those outside the Homes would miss his helping hand and again this year every widow, aged man and woman received coal and a liberal distribution of tea (in which the inmates shared) and money given to all the sick and under medical care."

On August 27th 1909 at the age of 85 this good friend of Ashwell's aged poor died. After bequests to his many relatives and servants, he left certain monies to the following: the Church Army, the Deptford Fund, the National Incorporated Association for the Reclamation of Destitute Waif Children, commonly known as Dr. Barnardo's, and the Soldiers' and Sailors' Families Association.

The poor boy from Ashwell had certainly made good, to the tune of £94,974.2.0d. Many years ago that fount of local knowledge, Henry Bowman, told me that George Moss invited everyone who was anyone to attend the foundation stone laying ceremony. Only one man refused, a stipendiary magistrate, who was also a director of one of the railways. He "did not wish to appear with this labourer's son who had made his money by some devious means". It is easy now to see how George's success might have been twisted into the story of the coffee stall.

Boer War heroes

Twice every Sunday for fifty-one weeks each year, the Rev. S.W.P. Webb preached at Ashwell church: the fifty-second week he spent with his wife Hattie at the seaside resort of Bognor; that was before King George the Fifth said a certain word and the resort became Bognor Regis.

As the little rector climbed the pulpit steps, stood on the stained and varnished margarine box and commenced his long sermon, John Hankin, one of the older choristers, settled down for forty winks and the boys in the front rows of the choir stalls tried to think of something to pass away the next half hour: whispering was forbidden; comics were not allowed in those days; but, occasionally, the monotony would be relieved when a sparrow took the wrong turning and flew into church. We would watch as it flew the length of the building, came to rest on one of the window sills then, after a few cheeky chirps, was off again crashing into the lattice windows in a vain attempt to escape the sermon.

I had read the inscriptions on the wall monuments over and over again. "Townsend Andrews LL.B., 42 years vicar of this parish. The Rev. Henry Morice M.A., Prebendary of Lincoln and for 39 years vicar of this parish". Then came the Rev. H.W. Hodgson (the first rector) who stayed for 41 years followed by the Rev. Samuel William Panajotti Webb who died in 1925 after 33 years at Ashwell. These four spent no less than a total of 155 years preaching the gospel to the people of Ashwell.

There was one monument fixed about ten feet high near the chancel arch. Fumes from the paraffin oil lamps had given the copper plaque a beautiful green patina but had also made it difficult to read. "The City of London Imperial Volunteers. In Memory of Gilbert William Cooper, a Private in this Regiment and also in this 4th Volunteer Battalion Essex Regiment. Son of William and Ellen Cooper of this Parish, he died at Cape Town on the Tenth of March 1900, during the South African Campaign, aged 20 years."

The discovery of gold in Johannesburg and other towns attracted many from overseas including English, but the Boer government in the Transvaal would not give them political rights. Known as "Outlanders", they decided after trying persuasion, to get by force what they wanted. With the approval of Cecil Rhodes who was at that time Premier of the Cape Colony, Dr Jameson, the Administrator of Rhodesia, set out from Mafeking with a force of 500 men to support the "Reformers". This raiding force reached Krugersdorp on 1st January 1896 where they were met by a strong party of Boers who forced them to surrender. Dr. Jameson was sent home under arrest, together with some English officers who had helped him; they were accused of invading a friendly state and were imprisoned. The British government then tried to persuade the Boers to come to terms with the Outlanders. In 1899 President Kruger offered them a sort of franchise, but with difficult conditions. The offer was rejected and war declared; troops were sent in from India but it took 250,000 men, composed of British, Colonials and volunteers, two and a half years to conquer 50,000 Boers.

Much of the fighting took place in Northern Natal; one town became famous, Ladysmith, founded in 1851 and named after Lady Juana the wife of Sir Harry Smith, Governor of Cape Colony. Ladysmith was besieged by the Boers from November 1899 until the end of February 1900, when the town was relieved by Sir Redvers Buller. Whilst Charles Gallant, an Ashwell soldier, was fighting at the siege of Ladysmith, his wife gave birth to a daughter; the mother proudly named her Alice Natalie Ladysmith Gallant. At about the same time the Ward family produced a son: he was named Redvers Ward.

Percy Dellar returned to Ashwell from the Boer War having lost one arm and two fingers from his left hand. For some years he was dressed and fed by his mother, but gradually he overcame his disabilities and, with time to spare, became a good cyclist and a very keen student of nature - birds, hares and rabbits, their habits, nesting and roosting places and how they were affected by wind and rain. Percy next bought a folding gun and taught himself anew to shoot, with the thumb and two fingers. Henry Bonnet the tailor made the clothes designed by Percy with special pockets to receive not only the gun but hares and pheasants.

Percy Dellar was probably the most scientific poacher Ashwell had ever known. When in the early 1920s the Ashwell Men's Club was formed Percy was one of the first to join. Old members still tell of his dexterity at cards, the hand of cards gripped between his knees leaving the thumb and two fingers free to place his card on the table.

He died in 1964 aged 83 years.

The "Hertfordshire Express" of 10th December 1899 tells the story of another of Ashwell's Boer war soldiers. "A romantic illustration of the separation of lovers caused by the war comes from the village of Ashwell. A reservist who was summoned to rejoin his regiment received the order at the most interesting moment of his life. He was not only engaged to be married, but the banns had been put up and the parson had got as far as the "second time of asking". The third "time of asking" was due in fact on Sunday.

"The couple were determined to wed, however, and so on Sunday at the close of the service at which the banns had been proclaimed a third time, the marriage took place. The honeymoon was short enough, for on Monday morning the husband had to start for Bedford, en route for the Cape. The names of this now celebrated couple are or rather were William Wilkins and Rose Westerman, both of whom (said a correspondent) are well known and highly respected in Ashwell. The rector, the Rev. S.W.P. Webb, officiated. There was a good attendance at church. The bells were rung twice during the day in honour of the event."

Documents at Ashwell Museum show that Private Wilkins served 10 years 43 days in the army and 2 years 322 days on reserve.

War: its memories and memorial

While the men were away during World War One, boys in the rural areas were allowed to leave school at the age of twelve. Even younger boys were employed to help in the harvest field in the long summer holidays. In August and September of 1917, when I was six, I worked for several weeks as a "shock boy". This was before the arrival of the internal combustion engine and farms were fully mechanised; the men had cut a narrow strip of corn round the edge of the field with scythes, then the horse-drawn Massey Harris self-binder had cut and tied the rest of the crop into sheaves. The harvest men then stood the sheaves up in "shocks".

It was at this point that Franz, Wilhelm and I came in. I led a horse pulling a cart from shock to shock, while Wilhelm pitched the sheaves with a fork up to Franz, who stacked them until the cart was loaded. By this time another horse and cart had arrived, brought by an older boy, who then led away our full load.

I should explain, Franz and Wilhelm were German soldiers; they wore grey uniforms with little round caps, spoke only a little English, but were very kind to me. They lived at the prisoner of war camp, the Maltings now converted into flats. The prisoners were marched out, under guard, to work for the farmers.

One of the prisoners collapsed and died while being taken to work; there was a large blood stain on the road at West End for several days. An oak cross was placed over the grave at the cemetery and from time to time someone placed a jam jar filled with flowers on the grave.

A favourite Sunday afternoon walk at this time was to the Therfield flying ground where, if we were lucky, it was possible to see the flying machines take off or land. There was great excitement when one crashed in a field at Newnham Bottom. We were able to examine it in detail, the wooden propellor, the yards of wire and metal tubing, the canvas-covered wings; we collected souvenirs with our pocket knives.

Edward Holloway, a pilot in the Royal Flying Corps, flew home and landed safely in a meadow at Loves farm; the news spread and scores of people dashed off to see the plane, among them my grandmother, who was in such a hurry that she fell and broke her wrist. My mother was called in to help because there was so much to do in that household, three bachelor sons at home, still too young to be called up for the war; there were parcels to send and letters to write and answer from her four sons at the war.

There was her third daughter living near Hitchin, and the eldest son at Baldock, but most of the work fell on my mother, who was married to another of the nine sons; if my arithmetic is correct, that accounts for the twelve children. My grandparents lived in a thatched cottage at West End.

While my mother was making beds, doing up parcels etc., my grandmother often sent me to Jack Worboys' shop in Back Street. Here you could buy anything from a packet of pins to a side of bacon, or half a pig in peace time. With rationing, Mrs. Worboys had brought in the sideline of selling second-hand clothes and odd bits of furniture. Jack was also bill-poster and Towncrier.

We had ration cards for meat, sugar, butter and things, but to boys it was the age of the cigarette card; those with lots of men relatives were lucky, or if you knew a publican's or shopkeeper's son, swapping was easy; cigarette packs were not sealed in those days!

At least one German Zeppelin flew over Ashwell; I remember my father covered our windows, then we went outside and watched it cruise towards London.

Mr. and Mrs. Wolverley Fordham went to live at Redlands Grange and gave up Ashwell Bury, so that it could be used as a hospital for wounded soldiers; a number of Ashwell ladies trained as volunteer nurses. The soldiers in their pale blue uniforms sat in the front pews at church on Sunday mornings.

In September, 1915, when I was four, one of my aunts married an Irish guardsman. Three things stand out in my mind about the occasion: my photograph was taken for the first time, there was trouble over the woman helper in the long white nightdress thing (she had sneaked in at the last minute, and stood next to my mother on the right) and this new Irish uncle gave me money, some of which I spent on too many penny bars of Fry's chocolate cream from Worboys' shop - they made me very sick!. It came to an end, of course, this war to end all wars. There was a bonfire and a procession. We all joined in and marched through the village with the great banner of the Ancient Order of Foresters at the head. Ashwell settled down as the men returned from the forces.

On the walls of the Merchant Taylors' School Mr. Chote had proudly hung photographs of his old boys in their uniforms, but the village felt there should be a more permanent memorial. There were those who thought it should take the form of a gatehouse chapel at the cemetery, others considered a stone cross more fitting. Plans for both were prepared and discussed and the Portland stone cross designed by Sir Edwin Lutyens won. The committee organised a house to house collection and the memorial was built.

On Sunday 4th December 1921, the church choir prepared for the solemn procession to the memorial service. On the wall of the vestry hung a roll of honour showing the names of 250 men who had fought in the war. Of these, nine were my uncles, two my cousins. Against the names of forty-two of them were the letters R.I.P, of whom three were my uncles.

A large body of people assembled for the service, the Right Hon. Viscount Hampden, K.C.B., C.M.G., who was to give the address, the Rector, the Rev. S.W.P. Webb, who was to dedicate the memorial and, last to arrive, Sir Herbert George Fordham, Kt., High Sheriff of Cambridge and Huntingdon, J.P. for Cambridge and Huntingdon, Deputy Lieutenant for Cambridge and Huntingdon and chairman of Cambridge County Council.

As the church clock struck half past two, Sir Herbert arrived, resplendent in his plumed hat, Deputy Lieutenant's uniform, sword clanking at his side. He had ridden down from his Odsey estate on his favourite steed, his Sunbeam bicycle.

The Brewery Outing

During the early years of this century, day trips to the seaside were organised annually by a number of firms for their employees and their wives. The railway company laid on a special train and, then as now, Yarmouth was a popular choice. One of the directors of Fordhams, the Ashwell brewers, overheard and recorded this tale as one of the employees told it.

"Ah me! that was a day, when the Master sent us all to the seaside. I never had such a day, nor did my Missus. Why, we was up at three and was to be at the station at four. All the brewery men, carters and all went and some had their Missus as well. We was a trainload and had some fun on the way down. No need to be thirsty, for an eighteen gallon cask was put in each end of the train and all you had to do when you wanted a drink was to pass a pot down to be filled. It was real amusing to see it. If you put your head out of the window, you could see the pot going carriage by carriage till it got where the cask was, then you could see it coming back, carriage by carriage to where he was as wanted the drink; it was real amusing. Both casks was empty when we got to Yarmouth, but there is a brewery there, and the Master got the casks filled up again afore we set off home, and we drank 'em empty again.

"We got there a little after ten and all went down to where the sea was. I never seen so much water afore in all my days, nor hant my Missus. Lor! I could hardly believe my sight and it all the while kep' muddlin' about. Some went one way and some another. Some sot in a public all day while it was time to start back home, there were several publics there, same as here.

"Me and my missus, we walked on the bank of stones where the water started from. It's a pity we haven't got a bank of stones like that here; good for roads they'd be. There was a boat a goin' on the water; Tom and Will Rob they was both in ready, so was the cook from the Master's house and several more. John Lee, he was in and I said I'd go. My Missus wouldn't and begged me not to go, but I would and did.

"That took ever so many folk to get the boat off the stones before she'd float, but in time she went a slidin' off pretty. Tom and Will they soon began singing and holloring the tunes what the organ with the flying horses played at the feast, but they didn't keep it up long. When we got a little way from the bank, the two men what belonged to the boat, they pulled two cloths, like two rick cloths almost up on to two poles which stuck up in the boat; when they got these cloths up, bless me how the wind did make them flucker about like you see wash cloths on a line, but soon the wind come and filled up them cloths till they bellied out, and then we went flying off through the water, straight as a bird. The water looked like milk behind us.

"John he was frightened. 'Put me ashore', he says. 'Oh no', says one of the men, 'You've come and you'll have to have your hour', so he had. Well, he soon began to look wonderful green he did and hanged his head over the side of the boat, when, lo and behold you, off comes Will's hat and away that floated. I says to one of the men I says 'Stop', I says, 'Here's a man's hat off'. He says, 'We can't stop. Where is it?' 'Gone in that direction', I says, and showed him over the off side. He never said no more.

"Presently I see him peeking with is hand up over his eyes like this here peeking, peeking he kept, so I says, 'What might you be a peeking after?' 'After that hat', he says. 'Oh', I says, 'That's the wrong way', I says, 'That hat dint go that way', I says, 'It's over this way'. He never said no more but after peeking he said to the other man what was sitting in the back end of the boat with a bit of wood under his arm, 'Ail her round', he says, and the other man pushes his bit of wood from towards the offside and lor' the cloths began to flucker again and the boat come ailing round as pretty and nice as nothing and off we went again in this direction this time.

"The man what was in the front of the boat, he got a pole with a little turned up spike on the end of it, and there he stood looking at the water. all in a sudden he shoved his pole in the water and lo and behold you, up comes Will's hat with the spike through it just in the top, that made a little hole in it, about as big enough to get your finger in. You can see it for yourself if you go up to Will's house. That was a new hat, new on that day, but however that man was able to tell where that hat was beats me. I see it go out, same as out here and he picked it up with his pole. That beats me that does. It was curious, but we seemed as if we was goin' up hill all the time and yet we wasn't.

"My Missus was glad to see me back again safe on the bank. I loved it I did, Will he didn't, more didn't Tom nor John, nor the Master's cook, none of them, only me. Deary me, thay was bad, green as green."

Philosopher's Gate

Charles Scrivener Walkden came to Ashwell in the late 1880s. He was an accountant with Fordhams the brewers, although he himself drank nothing stronger than ginger beer.

He is reported to have said: "One day Fordham's brewery will be nothing but a bed of stinging nettles".

The brewery has certainly gone; it was demolished in the 1960s, and a number of houses were built on the site, now known as Fordham Close.

According to another report, Walkden was asked when walking down Alms Lane the meaning of the initials and crest on the gable end of the parish room. Walkden explained that the initials R.F. stood for Rupert Fordham, who erected the building for use as a technical school, where evening classes could be held for working boys. The peacock, he said, was the crest of the Fordham family, and added: "The peacock is a vain bird with a small head".

Charles Walkden is remembered mainly for his herb business in Station Road, and especially for the "Philosopher's Gate". This was not an ornate wrought iron gate, but an ordinary five-bar gate, similar to many others, leading into fields and meadows. It was painted blue and white, and bore a number of strange Latin sentences in black. The top bar asked: "Where are you going?". The second bar warned: "Beware of the dog". The third bar: "And the ever watchful serpent". The fourth asked a very strange question: "Who shall guard the guards themselves?" The fifth bar gave an even stranger reply: "The evergreen". The left-hand post stated: "Knowledge conquers all things", and the right-hand post replied: "Nothing conquers knowledge".

Inside the gate was a field divided into plots where vegetables and herbs were grown.

Fifty yards back from the gate stood a collection of buildings, some close boarded, others with vents in the ends, which allowed the wind to dry the herbs, which were laid out on the racks inside.

This was the centre of one of Ashwell's small industries, where Charles Walkden employed two or three men to sort, dry and pack the herbs.

At this time men, women and children could be seen in the fields around Ashwell, collecting by the sackful coltsfoot leaves, burdock, wild rhubarb, silver moss, which grew freely in the sainfoin and clover fields, and dandelion roots. The latter were dug with a tool especially made by the local blacksmith. This was a type of fork with a single wide prong and a foot bar by which the tool was pressed into the soil to lever up the roots. A good example can be seen in the Ashwell Village Museum.

The demand for dandelion roots was so great that two Baldock men named Barker and Jellis brought donkey cart loads over to Ashwell.

In the late summer or early autumn the collectors turned to the hedgerows. One of the berries they sought was the privet used in the dye industry. The roots, leaves and berries were all carefully weighed by one of the Walkden employees, and the collectors were paid accordingly. After the drying processes the herbs were packed and sold to manufacturing chemists.

The Walkden family lived at Cliff House, Lime Kiln Lane, or as it is now known, Kingsland Way. They had three daughters and two sons. I have a press cutting of the 1940s from the Royston Crow which mentioned the Walkdens:

Mr Walkden collected money to have a handrail and steps to help people who had to carry water from the springs, he was a keen social worker and was largely responsible for the Technical building; he also worked hard to get allotments for working folk, [and] was the father of Mr. Percy Walkden, a Royston dignitary and zealous worker for the hospital. The other son, Alec, became Lord Walkden in the 1930s.

Under the pseudonym "Scrivener C. Scrivener", Charles Walkden wrote a book entitled Our Fields and Cities or Misdirected Industry, which was published by T. Fisher Unwin in 1891.

Among many other topics the book describes the Ashwell of those days:

"Daily newspapers are not kept for sale at Ashwell, they can be had by ordering in advance at the rate of eightpence a week each paper. One may however, see a daily paper in more than one of the seventeen public houses.

"The village boasts of some educational advantages. A school was endowed by one Henry Colborn in 1681, who charged the Merchant Taylors' Company with its management. The modern wardens of the ancient company visit Ashwell once a year to inspect their school. They travel in some style, the railway company has an express train stopped for them to alight from a saloon carriage. Another express train stopped to pick them up on the return journey. The church bells are rung when they enter the village and when they depart. The worthy Henry Colborn either forgot the girls or thought it unnecessary to educate them, or his instructions have been misunderstood. Fortunately for the girls, and for us and for posterity they are at a board school "managed" by five Ashwell people who meet once a month, without bell-ringing. Like other buildings in Hertfordshire this school, built in 1878, is in debt, it will be paid for by the year 1930, at least it is thought so.

"The parish consists of four thousand acres of fertile land, and some few properties in timber and thatch. There are also some rats. The springs are worth notice. About one hundred young people have migrated from Ashwell in the last ten years, three of them are now serving in the Army, twenty-six Ashwell men have retired from the Army and still live, thirteen of them in their native place, thirteen elsewhere. Population 1881: 1,568".

A School 'For Ever'

Two London Boy Scouts, out on an initiative test, came to ask me "How was the City of London connected with Ashwell in the seventeenth century?"

The answer is to be found inscribed on a stone tablet in Mill Street: "This school was built by the Merchant Taylors' Company of London, 1681, being the gift of Mr. Henry Colborn, late of London, scrivener, deceased. Edward Bushell (master), John Taylor, Robert Kaye, John Short, John Brett (wardens)."

The Scouts asked, as indeed do many visitors, "Who was Henry Colborn, and why did the Merchant Taylors build a school at Ashwell?"

Henry Colborn was a freeman of the City of London, steward and assistant of the Worshipful Company of Scriveners, or law writers. He died on 8th August, 1655, leaving lands and property in Ashwell among other places.

The will, dated 1st August, 1655, states: "If my son James die before twenty-one, or be married, the said lands, etc., in County Hertford shall be sold and the money given to such as I shall appoint by any codicil.

"To the Company of Merchant Taylors in London £1,000 to purchase lands for the erection of a Free Schoole and purchase land for an endowment and maintenance to be kept in Ashwell, Co. Hertford. To the said company £100 and also for the nomination of a schoolmaster there for ever."

The lands were sold, but produced only £701. 5. 0d. The master and wardens reported in 1665 that they had viewed a house at Ashwell but found "it will not be in any waies convenient for a schoole". They suggested that "leave might be procured from the Lord Bishop of Lincolne, that for the present the Schoole might be taught in the Chancell of the Church there".

At a cost of £290 the school was built in 1681, the charity being credited with the balance of £347. 10. 0d.

An official report of 1826 states: "This school has been entirely remodelled, and is now conducted upon the system of the National Schools. The premises consist of a neat Schoolhouse, with a garden and paddock attached.

"The old master, having from infirmity become incapable of discharging his duties, was allowed to retire last year, the Company allowing him a pension of £31. 10. 0d. per annum, being the full amount of his salary, and a new master was appointed at £40 per annum.

"The course of education is reading, writing and arithmetic, and about thirty poor children profit by the instruction thus afforded. The Schoolhouse and premises are now undergoing repair at the cost of the Company. Thus it appears that the funds of the charity have not only been faithfuly applied, but very considerably aided by the free bounty of the Merchant Taylors' Company."

In 1856 the rector and churchwardens proposed "that this opportunity be taken to record the thanks of the Vestry to the Merchant Taylors' Company for the great benefit the parish has derived from the excellent Grammar School they have established at Ashwell".

But in 1873 the vestry minutes record a letter from the clerk of the company: "The parish of Ashwell, having with every parish in England, to provide, under the Elementary Education Act of 1870, a school available for all children resident therein, this Court does not feel called upon to relieve the parishioners from such obligation, otherwise than by assenting to the use of Henry Colborn's Trust School".

The school failed to provide accommodation for 100 boys and, as a further stone tablet under the south window records, "This schoolroom was built and the old schoolroom altered at the cost of the Merchant Taylors' Company A.D. 1876".

The master and wardens came to inspect the new extension on 26th May. As the wagonette reached the entrance to the village the horses were removed, and willing hands pulled the party through the streets, preceded by the Ashwell brass band, followed by the headmaster, Mr. Chote, with his eighty-two pupils, and a large number of inhabitants. At intervals evergreen-covered arches spanned the streets, while the church bells pealed.

When in 1918 Mr. Chote retired the school walls were hung with photographs of his old boys in the uniforms of the Navy, Army and Royal Flying Corps.

Mr. Morgan Biles, a great cricketer, was headmaster from 1918, being followed by Mr. G.C. Whitby in 1933.

Mr. Whitby saw many changes. The Merchant Taylors became a senior mixed school, and 1939 brought evacuees, whole schools of them.

A third stone tablet in the entrance porch informs the visitor that the school finally closed in 1947 and is now a Further Education Centre and Ashwell branch of the Hertfordshire County Library.

The Architect's drawing of the Board Schools and Head Teacher's House in 1875, opened 1878. Note that there are two separate entrances for Juniors and Seniors. Later known as Ashwell Primary School. (Museum via Rev. J. Mullett)

The Merchant Taylors School in the 1920s (Author)

Boys at The Merchant Taylors School, 1908 (Museum/Howard Day)

A 1914 picture: Mr Chote the Headmaster is on the right, Mr Gale, a master on left. Taken in the school garden, the window on the right is now that of the village library at what is known as The Further Education Centre (Further Education Centre)

Merchant Taylors School Choir, Hertford 1923 (Author)
Back Row L to R: *Albert Sheldrick, Tom Marriot, Mr Biles, Tom Adkins, Frank Worboys, Denis Williamson, Stan Worboys, Harold Smyth, Cliff Gallant, Ted Bates, Reg Damant, Ben Game, Doug Smyth, Byron Searle.*
Kneeling: *C. Page, J. Geeves, F. Tyrell, W. Marriot, C. Oyston, F. Harradine, E. Harradine..*
On ground: *J. Davis, E. White, L. Bryant, P. Pettengell, C. Harradine, A. Baulk, F. Dilley, B. Simmons, J. Bray, W. Arthurs, W. Baulk, F. Brown, A. Webb, L. Bates, H. Waldeck.*

The classroom, new in 1876, was exactly the same in the 1920s, apart from an extra cupboard and photographs of Mr Chote's old boys in H.M.'s Forces.
(Museum)

Merchant Taylors School Orchestra 1936 (Museum)
Back Row: *Kathleen Cheetham, Alison Wylie, Olive Street, Mr G. Whitby, Roy Watler, Geoff Clarke, Kenneth Revel, Dorothy Furr.*
Second Row: *Peggy Cheetham, Mrs Whitby, Renee Watler, Iris Street, Bernard Hankin, Tom Wylie.*
Front Row: *Iris Hill, Mary Radford, Ronald Robins, Ben Seaby, Howard Day.*

The School in 1937 (Museum)
Back Row: *Mr G. Whitby, Iris Street, Renee Watler*
Fifth Row: *----?, Emily Livings, Mary Clements, Mary Radford, Marie Brookbanks, Bob Davies, Bert Skerman, Stanley Revill, Charlie Tyler.*
Fourth Row: *Mrs Whitby, Peggy Cheetham, Jane Dennis, Dorothy James, Ruby Hall, Aileen Mitchell, Helen Revel, Ted Eversden, Chris Clements, Alan Willatts, ----? Tyler, Ben Seaby, Arthur Livings, ----?, Howard Day.*
Third Row: *Nora Law, Hazel Skerman, Dorothy Furr, Sheila Picking, Joyce Westerman, Minnie Storey, Phyllis Willatts, Maurice Bird, Ken Revel, ----?, Ernest Hankin.*
Second Row: *Joan Skerman, Dorothy Andrews, Ruth Harradine, Sheila Picking, Alison Wylie, Mollie Moule, Tom Wylie, Nevill Albone, Sydney Cheetham, Eric White, James Smith.*
Front Row: Joyce Gurney, Gladys Hall, Pearl Harvey, Kathleen Cheetham, Joyce Collins, Jack Gifford, Ernie Booker, Taffy ----?, Harry Bullard.

Merchant Taylors pupils performing The Pedlar – *Open Air Theatre 1937. Note the girl with pigtails bottom left is Joyce Gurney. All the ladies wore hats.* (Museum)

The last Merchant Taylors pupils before the school closed in 1947 (Museum)
Back Row: *Margaret Hall, Doreen Milton, Alice Bryant, Evelyn Wilkins, Myrtle Seaby, M. Easter, Gloria Webb, Edna Skerman, -----?, Freda Bryant.*
Third Row: *Mrs G. Whitby (Headmistress), June Milton (School Secretary), Beryl Bryant, Edith Hayes, Pam Bryant, Bob Brown, Peter Chamberlain, Tony Huckle, Brian Walters, David Tweed, Dennis Moule, Vera Bryant, Joan Cole, Mr Farrier*
Second Row: *Daisy Clements, Barbara Hayes, Beryl Alcock, Eleanor Chamberlain, Mrs Leake, Gwen Moule, Mrs Vi Crack (the three school cooks), Cynthia George, Hilary Worboys, -----?, Barbara Worboys.*
Front Row: *Una Oyston, -----? Easter, Peter Hankin, Robert Sheldrick, John Spicer, Fred Bryant, Gerald Gallant, Michael Revels, Pauline Day, Olive Anderson.*

Many-talented Head

Towards the end of the 1918 summer school holiday Mr. and Mrs. Morgan Biles, with their daughters Gwendoline and Aline, moved into the school house in Mill Street for a stay of fifteen years. While Mrs. Biles and her daughters were settling in, Mr. Biles - with neatly trimmed beard, cloth cap and walking stick - took long walks, getting to know his new parish.

Miss Gwen Biles was an assistant teacher throughout the family's stay in Ashwell, while Miss Aline taught from time to time. Other teachers included Miss D.M. England; Mr. Joseph Clayton, who taught in frock-tailed coat, starched wing collar and cuffs; and shy Mr. Pickles.

In spite of the tremendous sums spent on education today, we are told that thousands of young people are unable to read or write. Whether the teaching methods of those days were superior to those used today I cannot say, but I do know that Morgan Biles and his team of teachers ensured that every boy could do both before he left school.

The method was simple and cheap. Reading and spelling from the Bible, the "Daily Mail", and the Children's Newspaper, together with the use of the blackboard and chalk. Writing from ancient copy books, the blackboard, slate and pencil, there was, of course, always the threat of the cane.

Mr. Firth of Royston took the woodwork classes, while gardening was supervised by Mr. Biles.

Mr. H.W. Bowman, a member of an old Ashwell family, came in from time to time to talk about history, and in 1921 he organised the beating the parish bounds. On the appointed day after assembly, the boys marched up to Carters pond to meet Miss A. Hyslop, headmistress of the Ashwell Girls' School, with her senior girls, there to be briefed by Mr. Bowman who carried a huge map of Ashwell. We were told that the parish contained 3,852 acres and was ten miles in circumference; that in ancient times it was the custom to examine the boundaries each year, and that the Ashwell churchwardens' accounts give the sums of money "layed out on beere and cakes when we did the perambulation". Our duties were to search out certain boundary posts and stumps, and as each one was found one of the younger boys was to be seized by two older boys, and bumped three times so that he would for ever remember his parish boundaries.

The beating began on the road to the Mordens at Paddocks, near the sheep dipping trenches, and continued along the parish and county boundaries until we reached Royston Way, where Sir George Fordham met the party and escorted it through the Odsey estate, over the railway track and on to the Icknield Way, where a halt was made at the Hare and Hounds for ginger beer and biscuits. On again to find the Bygrave boundary following Cat Ditch to Newnham boundary; then on to Caldecote, passing "Lousy Bush" - an ancient hawthorn tree overgrown with ivy - soon turning eastward along the Hinxworth boundary to the Cuckoo Inn, where we sat by the roadside to consult the map before the last long lap.

This followed the ditch towards Loves Farm, then northward over ditches, through green meadows, until the River Rhee was reached, passing Fan Mead, Harts Spring, the site of Howletts Mill, Labour in Vain Farm, Notch Close, Lord Meads Close, the old Forty Foot Way, Whitegate Common, and then Whitegate Bridge, a unique spot, because not only the four parishes of Dunton, Eyeworth, Guilden Morden and Ashwell meet here, but also the three counties of Bedfordshire, Cambridgeshire and Hertfordshire.

Leaving the bridge over the River Rhee, we changed direction again and followed another ditch past an overgrown moated site - the hillside where the Romans are said to have planted grapevines, still known as the Vineyard - back to the Morden road, where our beating had begun some eight hours before. Mr. T.B. Latchmore, a large jolly freckled and Norfolk jacketed photographer, cycled over from Hitchin with his huge camera, tripod and black cloth, to take photographs of us, and to examine the fossils and pieces of pottery collected at the school.

Percival Westell, the naturalist and curator of Letchworth Museum, was another frequent visitor, and we paid occasional visits to his museum, walking the two-and-half miles to the station and paying the fare to Letchworth. How we looked forward to the long-planned trip to the British Empire Exhibition at Wembley, and the choir festivals at Hertford, St. Albans, and Hitchin!

The village schoolmaster of those days had a difficult task - paper, pens nibs, even ink, were severely rationed, and the fires were watched lest the coal ran out before spring came. Sports and playground activities had to be organised.

Off duty Morgan Biles was church organist, and one of the best cricketers ever to play for Ashwell. When the Village Hall was opened, it was he who organised the Ashwell Choral and Dramatic Society, and found all sorts of talent in the most unexpected places. He was a member of the popular Ashwell Men's Club, and, of course, it was his influence on Neville and Jack Christy, Frank Dilly, John Bray and myself which resulted in our starting the Ashwell Village Museum.

Ashwell Water for Ashwell People

The estate agents' jargon "this sought after Hertfordshire village" may be true today but less than a century ago some Hertfordshire villages were much less sought after; in fact many of the inhabitants sought to get away.

In 1829 the Ashwell rating authority asked Cocket and Nash, a firm of Royston surveyors, to assess the houses and cottages of the village. The cottages are described very briefly: "Cottage stud and plastered with thatched roof, containing sitting room and pantry on the ground floor, two bedrooms above. The joint use of a barn and garden." The surveyor of today would enlarge on this report, "sitting room 11ft x 10ft, pantry 4ft x 3ft, floors of beaten earth, straw covered, delightful beamed ceilings with bedroom floorboards over, the whole tastefully limewashed. The stairs enter bedroom one 11ft x 6ft, second bedroom leads off first bedroom 11ft x 8ft. The joint use of privy or necessary which adjoins barn."

Of course the larger houses had better privies, some with mahogany seats; there were two-seaters fixed over a deep pit which was dug out from time to time. According to the "Royston Crow" of 8th May 1882, the Medical Officer of Health reported, "The old cesspit system prevails in this village, and I have found some very bad examples. There are, however, a few privies and troughs."

People everywhere had a great dread of fire; way back in 1632 the churchwardens had bought a "fire engeon" to fight the many fires. Most of the cottages, houses and other buildings were timber framed, thatched with local straw, so when the fire broke out it was extremely difficult to control. In extreme cases the two long fire hooks were brought from the church and attached to horses to demolish the adjoining property in an attempt to prevent the flames spreading.

Fourteen cottages were destroyed in the blaze of 1802, three badly burned in the 1844 fire and only six years later, on 2nd February 1850, came the biggest disaster of all, 'the Great Fire of Ashwell'. Thirty cottages, several tradesmen's houses and premises, seven farms, the Independent Chapel, the Quaker Meeting House and a Public House were destroyed, leaving two hundred people homeless.

The fire started about 11 p.m. towards the west end of Back Street where water could only be obtained from a few wells. Horsemen were sent to Baldock and Hitchin for help; it was after midnight when the Baldock brigade arrived and the flames were well on their way towards Jessamine House where, towards 4 a.m., the fire was halted, not far from Ashwell Springs.

The womenfolk in the Springs area found it easier to wash their clothes in the Springs pool rather than carry the water up to their homes and wash there. Foul drains and gullies from the surrounding properties had been craftily diverted into the Springs, and as Charles Walkden wrote in 1891: "the Springs are worth notice, the water from them is polluted before the sun has time to warm it". In 1855 the relieving officer found eight cottages sharing one privy, and that in a filthy state. Epidemics of scarlet fever, whooping cough and diphtheria were annual events. Between July 1884 and February 1885 there were 200 cases of smallpox and fever; 11 died of smallpox.

Ashwell was described as the most insanitary and disease-ridden parish in the area. The Medical Officer's report in 1886 found many of the wells were contaminated with sewage matter and unfit for drinking. So it was quite natural that numbers of young people sought to leave behind the cesspits and privies. Records show that in 1836 nine young men sailed for Canada; between 1841 and 1851 150 craftsmen and labourers left the parish and in the next ten years another 250. In 1891 Charles Walkden wrote: "About 100 young people have migrated from Ashwell in the last ten years, three are in the army, twenty-six have retired from the army and still live, three in Ashwell.

London, "the golden city", was a great attraction to the young at this time; they usually found a job before setting off, most of the girls to domestic service. Arthur Waldock, an Ashwell man, who became a buyer for a firm of fruit merchants at Spitalfields, told me that in 1900 he found nine people from Ashwell living in the Spitalfields area.

The year 1894 brought into being Ashwell Parish Council and Ashwell Rural District Council (consisting of Ashwell and nearby villages), the latter taking over the duties of the sanitary authority. Then 1897 brought a typhoid epidemic followed by a second in 1898, this time with fatalities. Surely this would bring a wind of change? The R.D.C. informed the Parish Council that the Local Government Board would now insist on improvements.

Under this pressure the Parish Council in 1902 obtained the advice of an engineer, whose scheme at a cost of £4,000, was for a complete water and sewerage works, the digging and boring of a well with pump-house and reservoir to supply the whole village and a sewage disposal area, to which new water closets would be connected through a main drainage system. In spite of village rows and pressure from the Local Government Board, the Parish Council temporarily shelved the scheme.

A public enquiry in 1903 settled the matter and in 1904 the sewerage works got under way. In 1905 Biggleswade Water Board offered to supply water for the whole of Ashwell Rural District. Then began a fight which lasted for five years. Edward King Fordham and the Rev. S.W.P. Webb for Biggleswade water, versus Henry William Bowman and James Rogers, "Ashwell water for Ashwell people". Henry Bowman argued that the Biggleswade scheme was more costly, its water polluted, and it caused goitre and furred up pipes.

In the run-up to the 1910 R.D.C. election Henry Bowman flooded the village with leaflets; he even carried bottles of Biggleswade and Ashwell water for the voters to sample. Bowman and Rogers were elected, but Ashwell people had to wait until 1914 before they were able to flush their closets with Ashwell water.

Ashwell Poets

Through the ages, the people of Ashwell have jotted down their thoughts on stone, brass, lead and paper. I have selected a few of the most interesting jottings.

When John Sell, a fifty-five-year-old Ashwell mercer, departed this life in 1618 someone wrote of him:

Aske how he liv'd and thou shalt know his end,
He dyed to God a saint. To poore a friend.

It was probably in the 18th century that the next four short lines appeared.

Ash'ell po'r people
Sot on the steeple
A crackin' o' meece
With a five farden beetle.

(Meece was the local pronunciation of mice. A beetle was a big wooden mallet.)

Thomas Everard cast these words in lead on the church roof:

Thomas Everard laid me here
He said to last an hundred year. 1714

Almost 200 years later the lead was renewed, but the good plumber's lines can still be read on the inner south wall of the tower.

In the 1850s Ashwell schoolchildren recited:

Ashwell is a pretty place.
It stands all in a valley.
There are six good ringing bells
Beside the bowling alley.*

(*The Six Bells public house, now the corner house at Church Path, had a bowling alley.)

The houses they stand thick and thin.
Young men there are in plenty.
Young ladies they can have their choice
For there ain't such a place in twenty.

God made man. Man made money.
God made bees. Bees made honey.
God made trees. Trees made branches.
God made young men To love little wenches.

Then in the 1870s came the Board school, and this poster appeared on the village notice boards.

To the School Board Electors of Ashwell

'Twas in sleepy, dirty Ashwell
In the Nineteenth Century
That a School Board was first thought of
By our worthy F.K.E.

Old Mills'son to gain favour,
(Of course he would, you know,)
With Math Thews for his toady,
Swore with the King they'd go.

But our good old Rectorodson,
Backed by a select few,
Said a School Board wasn't needed
And he'd tell them what to do.

But their actions were too honest
For Mills'sons' lot you know,
Such conduct they're not used to
Though they do to chapel go.

So hole and corner meeting
This old fox did connive,
And took with him his lackeys
To the King's place all alive.

But before the meet was over,
At least so I've been told,
A split was plainly manifest
Between these saintly souls.

And now we've got come forward
John Sale and Mr. Bacon,
With Mr. Hodgson, firm and true,
Who'll never be forsaken.

These gentlemen go publicly
And plainly speak their mind,
But not to secret meetings
Where the truth we cannot find.

So don't get taken in, ratepayers,
By the King or Mills'sons' lot
For if they once get into power
Why, you may go to pot.

And by their shifty ways
Pray do not be mistaken.
But give your vote to the three best men
The Rector, Sale and Bacon.

Vote for Hodgson, Sale and Bacon

Key: The King, (Mr. E.K. Fordham,) Mills'son, (the Rev. Millson, Congregational minister), Rectorodson, (Rev. Hodgson, rector of Ashwell).

From a faded purple booklet of twenty verses entitled "Ashwell St Mary's Church" written by Thomas Wylie,* I have selected the following four verses:

(*He came from Scotland about 1904 and farmed at Bear Farm for many years)

Some ashen trees; and water bubbling, springing
Just where the chalky hillside meets the plain:
And gathered all about them, clustering, clinging
The village homesteads have for ages lain.

Anon came messengers, with fateful story,
From lands afar, of faith and hope to be:
Of one who lived and died to bring to glory
The sons of men - the Christ of Galilee.

Then men arose of brain and finger crafty;
Who patient through the years upraised the shrine,
The columned aisle, the nave and chancel lofty,
And traceried window, to the Name Divine.

Far in the ages was the fabric founded,
Yet arch and mullioned window still are fair,
Far in the past were buffetings unbounded,
That lives of peace and freedom we might heir.

Then came 1914. Madeline Chote, who had taught seven-year-old boys at the Ashwell Merchant Taylors' School, watched them grow up, join His Majesty's Forces to fight in France, wrote a patriotic poem. After a copy had been accepted by Queen Alexandra, it was published in a national magazine. Here are three of the four verses:

We English Folk at Home

What can we do for England?
This isle of the silver sea.
This dear, dear land with wave washed strand.
Symbol of liberty.
Our men on sea and land go forth
To fight like sires of old.
They've said "Goodbye" to sweethearts - wives.
They're giving for England limbs and lives -
Is it much to give our gold?

Proud are we of England,
Of our Army's noble stand.
Of the stout hearts of our Navy,
The sure shield of our land.
Can we forget the heavy debt
To those brave sons we owe?
Louvain and Rheims "sermons in stone".
Women and children's piteous moans -
Homeless, helpless in battle zones.
We, here, are spared such woe.

How can we best serve England?
By garnering in each place
The richest wealth of the nation,
The children of our race.
To healthy frames teach mind and heart
Humanity's great plan.
Honour, Justice, Duty and Right,
Truth, Fair Play, Kindness, these unite
To form what "cultured Huns" would slight -
The brotherhood of man.

A fine view from the church tower – Claybush trees in the distance. The White building is 'King Dick's' house, now J. Cooke Engineering Ltd. Just below the Board Schools. Early 1930s. (The Author)

Left the Rectory and part of Churchyard. in the distance to the left, Dr Woodforde's house., The Mount, now Ashwell House. Early 1920s. (Peter Greener)

From the church tower, c.1935. (G.Shelton)
Bottom right Crumps Butchers shop, Workhouse Row, The Museum and Cottage garden.

From the church tower, c.1930. (G. Shelton)
Bottom right The Baptist Chapel. The long white block is Workhouse Row. Centre right is the Bury Gardens.

1930s. The junction of West End and Back Street. The boys are Roger and John Howes. The author's grandmother lived here. 20ft well discovered in the garden by present owner, Mike Buzzard in August 1991.
(Mr & Mrs P. Howes)

West End, c.1920
Farrows farm on left, on right part of Chantry House. George Robinson's cottage behind the hedge, now pulled down and replaced by Granta cottage.
(Robert Godsman)

Back Street, West End, early 1920s.
Note J. Lyons Tea van outside John Turkey Worboys' shop.
(Author)

High Street, c.1920. Left The Saddlery, pair of thatched cottages now demolished. The Courthouse of the Manor of Westbury Nurnuyts. J.H. Christy's shop. Right Bearfarm house. (Museum)

Ashwell Post Office, 1895. Postman Allan Waldock with beard. George Stanley who walked daily from Baldock to deliver the afternoon mail. Telegram boy William Holloway with bicycle. Frank Haylock, Ashwell postman. (Museum)

High Street, c.1910. The Post Office, The Rose & Crown, The Adelong. (Robert Godsman)

Left: The Two Brewers, The Stag, Fanny Adkins & Westrope's shop. Right: The Adelong, Day's bakers shop, The Guild House, with the Bulls Head in the distance. (Robert Godsman)

High Street, c.1905. The Bulls Head pub on left. On right Bonnetts the tailors now Plait Hall. (Peter Greener)

High Street, c.1905. Forresters Cottages right, entrance to Congregational Chapel on left. (Robert Godsman)

High Street, c.1905. The Three Tuns on left. On right Andersons shoeshop, Miss Bryants dressmakers house, Jessamine House. (Robert Godsman)

c.1905. The Recreation Ground on the right, The Cricketers Inn on the left. Named Elm Walk in the picture. Now Lucas Lane. (Robert Godsman)

Elbrook Lane, c.1920. Note the many elm trees, now gone. (Museum)

Silver Street, c.1900.
T.B. Latchmore

Mill Street, c.1920. Note the large stone to protect the corner of house from horses and carts. To the left now named Rollys Lane. (Museum)

Ashwell Village from Angell's Meadow, c.1920. On the right is the wall which surrounds the Quaker burial ground, and the footpath is the Quakers Walk.
(N.J. Gurney)

The Cage or Lock up, built about 1800 with stones from a demolished chapel on the north side of Ashwell church. The thatched cottage to the left was the Pindars Cottage, the land in foreground was the pound. Children in the picture – Chrissie Tyrell, George Page and Gwen Page..
(Author)

St Marys Church, c.1905.
(Robert Godsman)

Shops and plenty of them

Ashwell, before 1939, was the shopping centre for many people from the surrounding villages and hamlets. It was necessary for people to come to Ashwell to visit Doctor R.E.H. Woodforde, and J.R. Burton, the only chemist between Royston and Baldock. Certainly both Guilden Morden and Steeple Morden to the north-east had two small shops and about three pubs each. Guilden Morden also had the Harper family of bakers. Hinxworth to the west had its Horseshoes pub and the Kitcheners ran the small bakery, post office and shop, all in one. Newnham likewise to the west had only Mrs Lucas who sold tobacco and cigarettes from her front-room post office.

Neville Hine, its squire, would not allow a pub in Newnham, and Caldecote was too small for either shop, pub or post office. Bygrave was also rather bleak, although Mrs Clare sold cigarettes and twopenny packets of biscuits. Odsey had the Railway Inn, presided over by Mr & Mrs Bill Everitt, who not only sold beer, cigarettes, biscuits and crisps but had an ancient car for taxi work. Bill would don his peaked cap to drive visitors to Ashwell at a steady twenty to twenty-five miles an hour.

In those days the shopkeepers of Ashwell did quite well: between them they sold almost everything the householder needed. So having come into Ashwell from the far-flung corners of Doctor Woodforde's practice, survived the wait in the queue on the long gravel drive up to the surgery at the Mount, off High Street (opposite the Springs), sat on one of the three hard chairs in the waiting room, listened to the ailments of the previous patients as told to the doctor behind the glass screen, heard the mixing and shaking of the healing potion in each bottle, there was still time to do some shopping. (Important patients entered by the front door and waited in the dining room.)

The shops were open until 7 p.m., Friday until 8 p.m. and Saturday 8.30 or even 9 p.m. For small grocery items, or in summer if you fancied an icecream, Mrs Kirchin's was the nearest shop, in the front room of one of the pair of thatched cottages round by the Springs. A penny for a cornet; a large wafer of home-made icecream, vanilla, strawberry or chocolate cost twopence. Should you wish to have a bird or your favourite cat stuffed Arthur Kirchin was the man to see. After work as gardener to the Snow Fordhams at Elbrook House, he spent many hours as an amateur taxidermist.

There are several specimens of his work to be seen in Ashwell museum. But if it was boots or shoes you had brought for repair, bearded, white-haired, always smiling Tommy Knott was the man to see, in his repair shop next to the steps leading down to the Springs.

Should a lady wish to have a coat or dress made or indeed altered, prim little Miss Bryant (one of the Ashwell Strict Baptists) was the person to visit. Her front room next to Jessamine House was let on Thursday mornings to Barclays Bank so that local employers could collect the wages they would pay out on Friday night or Saturday morning. Now, sixty years later, Barclays Bank opens every morning from 10.00 am to 1.30 pm (but not Saturday) in the premises next door, which in Miss Bryant's day was a boot and shoe shop owned by Mr Anderson, a quiet, short, bearded man who was a sidesman at the Parish Church, and one of his daughters was a Sunday School Teacher.

Just round the corner in Kingsland Way was a sort of hole in the wall shop, where John Williamson, a big man who walked with a stick and wore a huge boot on one foot, sat repairing boots and shoes for the Andersons. For a few years during the twenties Arthur "Tart" Geeves ran a small fruit and confectionery shop from his tiny front room in Kingsland Terrace. On the north side of High Street opposite Miss Bryant's stood a feather edge boarded workshop, where Wilfred Bryant and Silas Worboys toiled at their trade as wheelwrights. If you needed a new wheelbarrow, a new cart or just repairs to either, this was the place to come. Both Wilfred and Silas were devout Wesleyan Methodists. As a local preacher, Silas walked many miles to preach at nearby village chapels. The cottage next to the wheelwrights' workshop was owned by Silas, and on one occasion during the twenties he and his daughter Irene had a tremendous shock when a farm horse complete with cart crashed into their living room. The horse had taken fright while travelling down steep Kingsland Way. The heavy cart, gaining momentum, had pushed the horse through the lath and plaster wall.

The village policeman lived next door to the Worboys for many years. When he retired, a young bachelor took over, and the police cottage was sold to Ebenezer Saunderson of Steeple Morden mill, who used it as a shop for the sale of chicken and pig foods. In those days, every other cottage had a hen house or pig sty, or both, in the back garden. Feed for animals attracted many rats and mice. After rain, the rats could be seen drinking in the rainwater gutters above the shop. When the brick floor under the Worboys' dining table sank, the bricks were lifted to disclose a large female rat with six youngsters. Another rat died under the bedroom floor leaving a nasty brown stain on the ceiling.

William Pack, farmer and blacksmith, lived in the house next to the Congregational chapel. The blacksmith's shop stood at the Silver Street end of this yard. At 7 o'clock each morning Bill Pack took a kettle of water to the forge, pumped at the bellows until the sparks flew, and soon the water was boiling for the first cup of tea. Bill made the iron tyres for Bryant's and Worboys' cart and barrow wheels. Apart from mending agricultural implements he had another sideline - a steam engine together with a threshing drum and chaffcutter which he hired out to local farmers during the autumn and winter to thresh the corn direct from stacks.

Two doors further on, Phil Cook opened a cycle agent's business. In 1928, I had sixpence change from £7 when Phil sold me a new Raleigh bicycle. The Victorian three storey building just across the street housed C.H. Westrope's grocery and drapery business. The grocery, provisions, wines, spirits, cigarette and paraffin oil side was run by Charles Westrope, a keen cricketer, parish councillor and organist at the Congregational chapel. Next came Mr Peters who cycled round the villages collecting orders from those customers who chose to have their goods delivered the following day by Frank Albone. There was also a boy who made deliveries on the trade bicycle round the village.

A pleasant aroma met you in Westrope's shop, a mixture of hand-ground coffee, tobacco, oranges and bananas; Tate & Lyle's granulated sugar in strong wooden boxes waiting to be weighed into dark blue paper bags; raisins and currants, prunes and all the good things were sold in those days without colourings, sodium glutamate and other mysterious additives.

Mrs Victoria Westrope, the widowed mother of Charles, a tall, upright lady dressed smartly in black, was responsible for the drapery side of the business ably assisted by Miss Hoy, also in black and wearing a wig. Drapery consisted of rolls of cotton and linen materials (which were measured for the customer on the brass yardstick screwed to the counter top), ladies' underwear, cottons, silks, wools, tapes, pins and needles, lisle and woollen stockings and various sidelines.

Next in the High Street came the Chemist's shop with bottles of Brylcream, Eno's and Kruschen salts, tins of Glaxo, Sanatogen, Gibbs solid dentifrice, Pears transparent soap and coal tar soap, embrocations and wintergreen oils. On the shelves behind the counter stood row after row of brown glass bottles bearing mysterious Latin names, containing the powders and tinctures which, mixed together and well shaken in a bottle marked off in tablespoons, cured the patients of the bearded Dr Woodforde; and in the window were two of those huge bottles containing one blue liquid, the other red, which for many years had been the sign of the chemist.

I am indebted to the late George Shelton for much of the history of the chemists and the Ashwell chemist's shop. The Shelton family lived next door and George started his career in this shop, later moving to Luton and in due course having his own chemists' shops.

G.W. Harrison is believed, however, to have been Ashwell's first chemist when this block of buildings was built around the middle of last century. At a time when head lice were widespread, there were many remedies, but Harrison's Pomade was regarded as the most efficient in destroying lice and their eggs. In a loft over the stable, entered by a ladder from outside, he also manufactured rat poison from phosphorus. Great care was necessary due to the inflammable nature of the phosphorus, which was stored under water at the bottom of the garden. Eventually Harrison moved to Reading where he carried on a very successful manufacturing business. The green tins of Harrison's Pomade became familiar in almost every household in Britain, until hygiene and hair care almost eliminated head lice.

Harrison was followed by Bond Smith who is said to have run the Ashwell chemist's shop as a branch of his Potton business. Around 1896 W.H. Bridgeman managed the shop for a time, before taking full ownership. He was a very clever chemist who introduced a range of veterinary products which included Anglo-American pig powders and a fly powder for sheep scab. These were advertised in the "Farmer and Stockbreeder" and other papers. Mrs Bridgeman contracted T.B. and died early in 1906; she was buried in the churchyard near the Hodwell fence so that her husband could see from a mound in his garden the marble cross erected to her memory. Bridgeman died later that year, also of T.B., and was buried beside his wife.

Next came E.T. Dukes, reported to be a good chemist who had a weakness for "the bottle". In 1913 he sold the business to J.R. Burton, still remembered by some of Ashwell's older residents today. J.R. carried on producing some of Bridgeman's medicines. I remember Burton's "B" Syrup, the B referring to Bridgeman; it was guaranteed to cure coughs, colds and other things. Jack Burton, as he became known, wore very thick lenses. He married the sister of blacksmith Jim Pack whose smithy stood next to Fanny Adkins' shop. J.R. was in the parish church choir and a prominent member of Ashwell Choral and Dramatic Society. He sold the business to E.E. Russell, the Letchworth and District chemists, but stayed on to manage the shop for a few years before moving to Forest Gate.

Adjoining the chemist's shop in one room of Ventnor House was John Ashwell's Butcher's shop, and in the back garden, facing the Rectory, a modern Slaughter-house.

Plait Hall was occupied by the tailoring family of Bonnett; the room next to Church Lane was the tailors' shop, and here Henry and his sons, Jim and Douglas, could be seen sitting cross-legged on the deal tables. In 1928 the Bonnetts made a suit which cost me just over £5. During one of my visits for a fitting, a Hinxworth man named Sale brought in a blue reefer jacket for repairs; the Bonnett family had made the jacket 50 years before! Mrs Bonnett made funny faces when her dentures slipped; she also taught the piano. She and her husband were strict Baptists. Two sons were keen local historians.

Mrs Bonnett was the organist at Zoar Strict Baptist Chapel in Gardiners Lane for many years. On 3rd September 1939 she did not appear at the beginning of the morning service, so 10 year old Norman Gurney took over. Halfway through the service she suddenly appeared, and announced that war had been declared. She never played the organ again.

Mrs Bonnett's playing was particularly notable for the clicking sounds which accompanied it, due to the many rings she wore on her fingers!

Window to Watch

Across the street stood the old Bull's Head, part of which was used as a Greengrocer's shop by Mrs Dilley, the other end, next to Bulls Head twitchell (alley), was Miss Winnie Stamford's Wool shop. The red brick building opposite was once a wonderful shop, owned by Miss Fanny Adkins, a genuine Victorian lady, always dressed in black, with a long dangling necklace, spectacles low down on her nose, so that she could look over the top, and finally a pencil stuck in the plaited hair on top of her head. You name it, Fanny sold it - from a halfpenny packet of pins to half-crown Ingersoll pocket watches, tin kettles and saucepans, penny postcard views of Ashwell (made in Bavaria), hats, balls of string, socks and stockings, button-sided boots and spare buttons for the same in little round wooden pill boxes; black, white and red lace, with scores of patterns to choose from; cottons and silks, rolls of cloth and so on.

During the weeks leading up to Christmas, Fanny Adkins' window was definitely the window to watch. Every day after tea, except Sunday when the blue roller blind was lowered, children were there, noses pressed against the cold plate glass window, looking longingly at the wonderful display. For among the tinsel and coloured paper chains, illuminated by a hanging lamp, were clockwork motor cars, and clowns, leaden toy soldiers, sugar mice, marbles and skipping ropes, peg tops and humming tops, ludo, snakes and ladders and boxes of crackers, crayons and paints, magic slates, drawing books, story books, John Bull printing sets, dolls tea sets, dolls large and dolls small, dolls dressed and dolls undressed. As the great day drew nearer, one by one the best toys were removed from the window and those of us who knew the identity of Father Christmas realised that someone's parents, uncles or aunts had bought someone's Christmas present.

Blacksmith James Pack lived next door to Miss Adkins' shop. When the Packs left Ashwell the premises were taken over by Mr and Mrs Alfred Ketteridge. Very soon a huge tank was sunk into the yard, with a hand-operated pump above it and the strange name "Pratt's Ethyl" stencilled on the white globe. Ashwell's first garage had opened.

The Ketteridges did repairs and taxi work, and later bought a 20-seater coach made by Crossley's. This was in great demand.

I remember a church choir outing to Yarmouth and a school trip to the British Empire Exhibition at Wembley in 1924. For several months we had taken pennies to school to pay for the coach fare and entrance fee. It was a marvellous exhibition: the palace of engineering, coal mine complete with cage, sheep being shorn in the Australian pavilion, prospectors actually panning for gold in a pool of dirty water. New Zealand, Canada, India, Africa - the whole Empire was there - as well as a huge funfair. Ashwell fair seemed very dull after that, in spite of the two days' school holiday!

Across the street, widow Mrs Searle ran a baker's shop with her daughter Dorothy and son Byron who delivered bread by bicycle to a small number of customers. Later the shop was taken over by Bert Collis, whose special lines were bicycles, gramophones, tobacco and confectionery.

Adjoining Mrs Searle's shop was a block of cottages with another shop at the other end, the name board over the window clearly stating Day, Baker & Confectioner. Apparently, Days started their bakery at Baldock in 1714, and took over the present Ashwell premises a century later. During the 1920s the head of the family was Leopold Day, a tall, bearded man who rode a tricycle and seemed to take more interest in his poultry runs near the Engine Public House in Back Street than he did in the bakery business. Motherly old Mrs Leopold, after bearing sixteen children, served in the shop with daughters, Kate and Mary. Son Charles with his son, also named Charles, baked in the coal fired ovens. Charles senior, known as Old Charley, always dressed very smartly, with a gold Albert watch chain hung across his waistcoat and a gold £2 piece hanging from the centre. Apart from being a parish councillor and rural district councillor he was well known as the Chairman of North Herts Coursing Club. The whole block of property was owned by a strange man, a chemist known as "Barmy Mathews", whose shop, with its dirty windows hiding the goods on display, was one of the sights of Royston High Street. From time to time he would appear in the shop doorway with long matted hair and filthy clothes.

But I digress. Back to High Street, Ashwell, where Mathews' property had become sadly neglected, plaster falling from the walls and paint peeling off the doors and window frames. As he refused to pay his rates to Ashwell Rural District Council, the magistrates from time to time ordered that certain of his goods and chattels be sold.

I have a press photograph of 1937 with a caption below stating, "These Tudor cottages are threatened with demolition, but efforts are being made to preserve them". Barmey Ernest Mathews passed on, to wherever chemists go, and his nephew sold the cottages to the late Mrs J.D. Beresford and the baker's shop and premises to the Day family. In spite of threats of demolition from council officials, it is to these two families that Ashwell owes the restoration of what is recognised as the Guild House or Hall of the Fraternity of St John the Baptist, the Guild having been re-established in Ashwell in 1476.

Opposite Day's shop stood the Stag's Head Public House. Mrs Covington, the one-eyed landlady, sprinkled fine sand on the boarded floor especially for those customers who missed the black-leaded cast-iron spittoons which stood in each corner of the bar. After her death, the brewers closed the pub and the premises became a branch of Letchworth, Hitchin & District Co-operative Society selling groceries etc and remained so until the 50s when it was converted into two houses. On the other side of Alms Lane in another converted pub, the Two Brewers, lived widowed Mrs Dellar who had a green-grocery and second-hand furniture business with two of her sons, Percy, and Charles who was, I believe, born a cripple. The latter set out every morning with his horse-drawn van loaded with fruit, vegetables and chickens. On the road to Newnham he would pluck the chickens, leaving a trail of feathers! Charley was so well known in the village and in Baldock and Letchworth Garden City, that the customers came out to buy from the van, while he rested his crippled legs and lit one Woodbine cigarette from another.

When one of his horses died he was persuaded to buy a mule, probably one left over from the war. The mule was really obstinate. When it came to a hill, it just refused to move, so Charley found it necessary to employ a helper, who devised a clever trick. As they were nearing a hill an old waistcoat was hung over the mule's ears by the armholes, thus blindfolding the animal; then a few sharp cracks of the whip and the hill was conquered.

Eventually Mrs Dellar gave up the business and it became a shop for the sale of fruit, tobacco, cigarettes and confectionery, with Mr and Mrs George Holloway in charge.

Next door lived blacksmith William Bean and son Jim. Whilst the father was a small man, Jim was big and strong; in fact so strong that when father William was holding a piece of red-hot iron on the anvil for Jim to hammer into shape, the old man would often shout "lightly Jim, you'll break the bloody anvil", much to the amusement of the schoolboys watching over the half door of the blacksmith's shop. Jim Bean's other claim to fame was that he was the only man known to have walked from Portsmouth to Ashwell. In his youth, Jim went on a day's rail excursion to Portsmouth and missed the return train. Having spent all his pocket money, he decided to walk home. There were those who said Jim had tried to join the navy, others thought it more likely that he had been overcome by the strength of Brickwood's Portsmouth ales.

One of an old Ashwell family, Les Worboys lost a leg in the 1914-18 war, then trained as a boot and shoe repairer and opened up a tiny shop opposite the blacksmith, next door to the Rose and Crown Inn.

On the west side of this Inn was A. & C. Christy's coal merchants, mineral water manufacturers and newsagents. The coal and mineral water side of the business was run by the brothers Frank and Percy Christy. Unlike the majority of brewers, E.K. & H. Fordham, the Ashwell brewers, did not supply their licensees with mineral waters and soda water, leaving this quite profitable side to the Christys. People could purchase direct from the factory a dozen bottles of mixed mineral waters for eighteen pence. The range included lemonade, ginger beer, cherry cider, American ice cream soda and football stout; other Christy products were soda water in Christy's own labelled siphons and ginger wine.

They were also agents for Smiths Crisps, with the little blue twist of salt, and nuts and raisins, both at twopence a packet. Frank and Percy spent most mornings cycling round Ashwell's eleven pubs - for business reasons of course - while back at the coal yard Arthur Goss drove the old solid-tyred Ford lorry up to Ashwell station, shovelled on a load of coal from one of Christy's coal trucks, picked up the bundles of daily newspapers and brought them back for Miss Nelly Christy and her assistant, Miss Queenie Parkhouse, to sort out for the morning delivery round.

Fanny Adkins shop & house in 1895. Until 1990, was the Village Surgery. Apart from the wonderful display of goods & chattels note the church tower, minus clock faces. The Six Bells pub then owned by Hudsons brewers of Pampisford; in the 1920s owned by Pages brewery of Ashwell, at the bottom of Church Lane. The delivery boy is probably Ralph Covington, and Fanny herself the left hand figure in the window.
(Dr F. Moynihan)

M.V. Crump's the butchers shop in 1930. (M.V. Crump)
Left to right: George Arthur, Mark Crump and Gordon White.

Tommy Dennis's shop with its unique topiary and Bulls Head. Mr Dennis (left) with Mark Crump. The picture is probably 1950s, but the shop looked like this pre 1939.

Philip, Mark Crump's son, took over the business in 1954 and now his sons David and Jonathan are in charge. (M.V. Crump)

A familiar sight in Ashwell before 1939. The boy on the front bicycle is probably Phil Crump. The original has been greatly enlarged so that the wording can just about be read – Ice Cream Tubs: 4d!!
(M.V. Crump)

Day's Bakers shop in the High Street, c.1925. Charles Day Senior with grandson Howard, recently retired, who greatly developed the business.
(Howard Day)

The Philosopher's Gate at the entrance to Charles Walkden's Herb Collecting business in Station Road, c.1920. Now the site of Peter Sheldrick's Taxi and Minibus Service.
(Peter Greener)

Searle's shop, Back Street, West End, c.1935, with Mrs Searle Sen., Byron's grandmother. The shop was originally owned by Jack Turkey Worboys. Jack was the Town Crier and Bill Sticker. Originally Mrs Searle ran a baker's shop in High Street, later Collis's shop. (Museum)

Collis's Cycle Shop. During World War II, various fund-raising efforts took place, in which processions played an important part. A Wurzel Gummidge figure dressed in straw has a placard "Who has our 66 Coupons", these referring to the clothes rationing. (Museum)

High Street, c.1914. (Museum)
Left George Strickland's Baker's shop, later Ernest Searle's, later Collis's Cycles etc. The rest of this block of property belonged to Barmy Mathews of Royston and was in a very bad state. It was later replastered, but in 1949 all the plaster was removed and the original timbers exposed. At the same time, Fred Bray and I repaired the plaster pargetry on the so-called Guild House. .

Westrope's shop front in the late 1890s. (Mrs G. Westrope)
The various aspects of this photograph overshadow the quality. Note: Gin 2/- a bottle.

Above left: *The Blacksmiths shop, c.1938, opposite the Rose & Crown.*
Above centre: *Almost next door, the shop owned by Mr & Mrs Searle, the former holding Byron in his arms, in 1937.* (Mr & Mrs B. Searle)
Above right: *Christys, Grocer and Draper, 1924, with Hector and Percy Pammenter. Now owned by a family from Punjab, who have also taken over Dennis's shop.* (Museum)

Left: *A 1939 picture of the Searle's shop, where now Barclays Bank operates. On the corner had been Anderson's, later Bonness' Boot and Shoe shop, and then Collis's General shop.* (Mr & Mrs B. Searle)

1903.

ASHWELL & DISTRICT

FLOWER SHOW & SPORTS.

THE SHOW

WILL BE HELD AT

ASHWELL

—ON—

Thursday, July 23rd, 1903,

BRASS BAND CONTEST.

EXECUTIVE COMMITTEE:

Chairman ... ... W. A. FORDHAM, ESQ.

Vice-Chairman... ... ...MR. J. H. ARROW,

MR. W. BOWLES, MR. J. PAGE,

„ W. H. BRIDGMAN, „ W. W. PACK,

„ R. W. CLARKE, „ S. PARKHOUSE,

MR. C. O. M'COY, *Hon. Treas.*

Hon. Sec.—**Mr. H. W. BOWMAN.**

MASON, PRINTER, ROYSTON.

I

Believe that the majority of Skin Eruptions, such as Blackheads, Pimples, Boils, etc., and such Skin Diseases as Eczema, etc., also Ænæmia, are much more prevalent at this time of the year than at any other. Irritation or soreness of the skin in whatever form it exists is painful to bear, and erruptions are unsightly. Ænæmia is most prevalent also and most persistent. The

LOVE

of life, is in proportion to the circumstances under which we exist. And if you are a sufferer from any skin disease that is painful to bear, or if your skin seems on fire or maybe you are suffering from shortness of breath, no energy and that collapsed condition produced by Ænæmia, how can you enjoy life to its full extent if you are in misery ?

YOU

can be quickly cured of all these complaints by taking Bridgman's Tonic

BLOOD PURIFIER

which soon produces rich blood & makes life worth living.

Price 1/- per bottle. Send for some if you suffer. Three bottles for 2/9 post free.

BRIDGMAN, **Pharmaceutical Chemist, ASHWELL, Herts.**

The Cover and some adverts from the Ashwell and District FLOWER SHOW & SPORTS, July 23rd, 1903. – I'd love to know where we can get Bridgman's Tonic! (Museum)

6

FANNY ADKINS, ASHWELL,

GENERAL STORES.

Latest Fashions. Lowest Prices.

New Stock Ladies' & Gent's Boots & Shoes.

Newest Millinery Trimmed and Untrimmed, Sailor Hats, Flowers, Feathers, Ribbons, Chiffons, Laces, Gloves and Hosiery, Corsets, Dress Material and Heavy Drapery, Clothing, etc.

Agent for Horniman's & Nelson's Pension Teas.

Always on show, Large Stock of Fancy Presents and Toys.

A LARGE ASSORTMENT OF PAPERHANGINGS.

T. A. FLITTON,

ASHWELL,

Locked Room for Cycles.

Sub-Agency for New Hudson Cycle Co.

Repairs. Free Inflation.

Fire and Accident Insurance Agent.

Cycles Stored 2d. each.

G. E. STREATHER,

Monumental Mason and Carver,

MELBOURN RD., ROYSTON.

MONUMENTS OF EVERY DESCRIPTION,

Either RED or GRAY GRANITE, MARBLE, or STONE.

Inscriptions Engraved in any style Imperishable Lead Lettering and Carving a Speciality.

BOOKS OF DESIGNS ON APPLICATION.

ESTIMATES GIVEN FOR EVERY DESCRIPTION OF MASON'S WORK.

4

Westrope's Stores.

DEPARTMENTS.

Dress Materials	Trimmings	Carpets
Prints	Laces	Floor-cloths & Linoleums
Mantles and Jackets	Embroideries	Cocoa Matting
Lace Curtains	Handkerchiefs	Hearth Rugs & Mats
Table Covers	Gloves	Ironmongery
Cretonnes	Umbrellas	Enamel Ware
Quilts	Hosiery	Trunks
Household and Table Linen	Haberdashery	Paper Hangings
Horrockses	Hats and Caps	Oils, Colours
Longcloths and Flannelettes	Men's Clothing	Paints and Brushes
Flannels & Blankets	Boy's Clothing	Grocery
Corsets	Boots and Shoes	Provisions
Ladies Underclothing	Sewing Machines	Wines & Spirits
Millinery	Stationery	Cigars and Tobaccos
Flowers and Feathers	Work Boxes	etc., etc.
Ribbons	Photo Frames	
	Household Furniture	
	Bedding	

High St., Ashwell.

G. Bryant,

FAMILY BUTCHER,

MILL ST.,

ASHWELL.

Beef, Mutton, Pork, Lamb, Veal of Prime Quality. Best Pork Sausages.

Families waited on Daily.

M. V. CRUMP,

Mill Street, ASHWELL,
Herts.

BEST HOME-KILLED MEAT ONLY.

Our Motto :—

ALWAYS THE SAME.

"Not how **CHEAP** but how **GOOD.**"

Quality lingers long after price is forgotten.

Purveyor to His Majesty's (Subjects).

SPECIALITIES :

PRESSED BEEF, BRAWN and SAUSAGES.

All TEAS are supplied at this Show by

C. DAY & SON,

Fancy Bread & Biscuit Baker,

Pastrycook, Confectioner and

Refreshment Contractor.

HIGH STREET, ASHWELL.

C. H. WESTROPE,

GROCER,

Provision and Wine Merchant,

Draper and Outfitter.

IN ALL DEPARTMENTS

QUALITY & SERVICE.

HIGH STREET, ASHWELL.

E. K. & H. FORDHAM,

LIMITED.

ASHWELL BREWERY,

HERTS.

Noted **ALES & STOUT**

In Cask and Bottle.

BASS & GUINNESS

Supplied in Bottles.

Private Trade Orders for home consumption specially attended to.

Gaymer's Celebrated Norfolk Cyder

Medium Sweet .... 7/6 per doz., Half Bottles.

Dry (Highly recommended) .... 9/- " "

Private customers supplied with 1 Dozen and upwards.

GAYMER'S CYDER was ordered for H.R.H. the Prince of Wales South African Cruise in H.M.S. "Republic," 1925.—Follow the Prince.

Attractions.

Criers From Old London.

CAMBRIDGE ALBION BAND.

Stalls and Sideshows.

Hoop-la. Pocket Your Prize. Revolving Horse.

Felix the Cat. Game Plane. Electric Board.

Potting for Pig. Cocoanut Shies. Goal Kick.

CYCLE GIVEN AWAY.

Dancing from 8 p.m. to 9.30 p.m.

9.30 to 10. FIREWORKS. 9.30 to 10.

TEAS supplied by C. DAY & SON, of Ashwell.

THE ASHWELL SADDLERY,

High Street, Ashwell.

ALL KINDS OF SADDLERY AND HARNESS SUPPLIED.

REPAIRS A SPECIALITY:

All work carried out by Experienced Workmen.

All kinds of Sports Requisites supplied.

Binder Twine and Hemp Cord always in stock.

Prices bear Competition. A Trial is earnestly Solicited.

BLUEGATE'S FARM DAIRY,

ASHWELL.

BEST QUALITY MILK SUPPLIED.

Pure Dairy Butter.

Fresh Cream Supplied Daily.

Milk produced under hygienic conditions.

Inspection invited of our Model Dairy and Cowsheds.

J. H. CHRISTY & SON,

Grocers and Drapers,

Earthenware, Hardware & General Stores.

Established over a Century.

High Street :: ASHWELL.

"THREE TUNS" Hotel,

ASHWELL.

Luncheons :: Teas :: Dinners.

Garage, Stabling, Etc.

Proprietor—H. BENTLEY.

F. DILLEY,

"ROSE & CROWN"

ASHWELL.

All kinds of WINES and SPIRITS in Stock.

SIMPSON'S FINE ALES AND STOUT.

BASS and GUINNESS in Bottles.

LUNCHEONS AND TEAS. STABLING ACCOMMODATION AND GARAGE.

"The Bushel & Strike"

(Under New Management)

Mill Street, ASHWELL.

Proprietor : Walter Parry.

All Kinds of WINES and SPIRITS.

E. K. & H. FORDHAM'S Fine **ALES & STOUT.**

Bass and Guinness in Bottles.

Luncheons & Teas provided. Good Stabling Accommodation

Motorists and Cyclists Catered for.

Some adverts and attractions of the 1925 August Bank Holiday Show.
(Museum)

More Ashwell entrepreneurs

The hub of the Christy empire was to be found in the little Post Office and Newsagents shop next to short Bear Lane. It was here that Nelly, the sister of the Christy brothers, ran the whole concern. Here you could place an order for mineral waters, coal, coke, anthracite, daily newspapers (the Labour "Daily Herald" was kept under the counter), weekly magazines, etc. The usual brands of stationery were stocked, with pens, pencils, postcards and rubbers, blotting paper, etc. It was a very busy shop. Although the post office didn't stock Postman Pat and some things found in post offices today, the two ladies were responsible for sorting the incoming mail and hand stamping the outgoing mail, stamps, postal orders, pensions and telegrams and, in addition, the telephone exchange was there in an adjoining room. Squeezed into one corner of the shop was Ashwell's only telephone call-box, housed in a dark stained and varnished box. The Shop is now a Dental Surgery, Ashwell being one of the first villages to have one.

Meanwhile, back at the yard Charley Burton, a bowler-hatted and sack-aproned little man, was busy filling coal sacks. Before the firm invested in motor transport Charley delivered the mineral waters to Fordhams pubs for several miles around by a horse-drawn van. In time, the horse became quite familiar with the regular routes, and if Charley had been offered a pint of beer at each of ten or more houses and just happened to nod off on the home-ward journey, the horse was quite capable of bringing him back safely.

After a late breakfast, Arthur Goss went back to load up the sacks of coal for delivery to the Ashwell and district customers. On one occasion, Arthur was involved in a slight accident on his way to load coal at the station sidings. The old Ford was doing at least ten miles an hour on the steep hill just before he reached the gamekeeper's house where John Kingsley, the farm bailiff, lived, when he saw Sir George Fordham pushing his bicycle up the hill. Mysteriously the solid tyred wheels of the Ford crushed the bicycle. Fortunately, Sir George escaped injury.

According to Arthur, Sir George had deliberately pushed the machine under the wheels of the lorry, which of course Sir George strongly denied. Unfortunately, or was it fortunately, the breathalyser had not been invented, because Arthur was very fond of a pint or two. On the other hand, Sir George was returning to Odsey after a morning's work at Ashwell brewery. As someone said "All's well that ends well" and so it was. Arthur was reprimanded and Christy's bought a handsome new bicycle fitted with an adjustable mirror on the right handlebar so that Sir George could keep his weather eye open for a dirty brown Ford lorry with solid tyres.

Spiritually, this branch of the Christy family had a foot in two camps. Mr and Mrs Frank and Mr and Mrs Percy were of the Congregational persuasion, while Miss Nelly was of the established Church; in fact she was a Sunday School teacher. Of course there were those who said this was a crafty move to encourage customers from both denominations.

On the other side of High Street facing A. & C. Christy's was the grocery and drapery store owned by another branch of the Christy family, J.H. Christy and Son. The Christys would seem to have come to Ashwell in the seventeenth century. John Christy was a little old man who pottered about in the shop and left the running of the grocery, provisions and ironmongery side to his son Harry, who was supported by Albert Covington, Hector and Percy Pammenter.

The drapery side was very efficiently organised by Harry's sister May, with Gladys Chalkley as second in command. Young Ashwell couples came to Christy's when they were about to be married. They would be taken up to the warehouse, where they could choose a tin kettle, enamelled or cast iron saucepans, baking tins, basins, crockery, cutlery, coconut matting, door-mats, pokers and coal shovels and tongs; blacklead brushes, boot brushes, scrubbing brushes and clothes brushes, enamel bowls, galvanised bowls, buckets or baths and garden tools. Down in the drapery section, May Christy would fit them out with towels and table cloths, sheets and pillow cases, blankets, etc.

These Christys were Church of England, and it was good for business. The Rector, the Rev. Samuel William Panajotti Webb, and Mrs Hattie Webb ran a monthly account for groceries and other provisions, paraffin oil and candles to light the rectory. The Church also had an account for brooms, brushes, cleaning and polishing materials, paraffin and candles not only for the Church but the room used for mothers' meetings, bible classes and whist drives known as the Technical Room. Each year J.H. Christy and Son donated several packets of candles to light up the church windows during harvest festival.

Most Ashwell people were C. of E. in the twenties, the Ashwell Fordhams, the Beresfords, Sales, the Westbury Christys, Angells, the Jim Packs, J.R. Burtons, the Days, Seymours and Barlees and, I almost forgot, Colonel and Mrs Ryder Wilson of Ringstead (late Indian Army), and of course the lower orders. (As Mrs Ryder Wilson often remarked, "Everyone who was anyone was there".)

There were many ladies who did not approve of Mrs Ryder Wilson's vivid and heavily made up face; in those days ladies, apart from ladies of the street, wore just a dab of powder and the merest hint of lipstick. However, the Wilsons had their part to play in the life of Ashwell, apart from the Parish Church. They were leaders of Ashwell and District Conservative and Unionist Association, for which the gardens at Ringstead were very useful, and their bull-nosed Morris Cowley was kept busy at elections. It was the custom for most of these good church people from time to time to invite the Rector and Mrs Webb to afternoon tea; for Mr and Mrs Harry Christy it had to be on Thursday, early closing day.

Most housewives did their own laundry, boiling clothes in a coal-fired copper and then wringing them through the wooden rollers of a mangle. Some used the services of either the Hitchin or Biggleswade laundries, whose vans collected and delivered weekly. A few used the smaller and less expensive local laundry run by Mrs Fred Gentle of Lucas Lane. Here, in a small outbuilding built of clay bats with a corrugated iron roof, Mrs Gentle boiled the clothes and then after they were carefully dried and ironed, husband Fred (always known as Timmy Gentle) returned them by two-wheeled hand cart in his spare time, after work at Fordham's brewery. The Gentles were very thrifty. Having purchased their own cottage they went on to buy the cottage just beyond the Cricketers, and later the pair of cottages with large premises, now called The Old Forge at the junction of Kingsland Way with Ashwell Street.

Just demobbed from the first World War, Thomas Disher Dennis, a young Potton butcher, decided that Ashwell needed a third butcher's shop. Having married Jessie, the daughter of blacksmith James Adams, Thomas persuaded his in-laws to allow him to open a shop in their front room, next door to Christy's, and put up a sign "T.D. Dennis, purveyor of British & Colonial meat". Deliveries at first were by bicycle, followed by a motorcycle with a large box in place of a sidecar. The business grew quickly and the shop expanded into Christy' office. A van took the place of the motor cycle, followed by a smart car and a second van. The shop front gradually took shape, with red steps, a fretted overhanging fascia with a bull's head with winking eyes in the centre plus two hanging baskets of lobelia and petunias, shaped box bushes at each end and masses of geraniums, all set off by gleaming white glazed tiles. It was described by some as the smartest butcher's shop in Hertfordshire, by others a blot on Ashwell's High Street.

Tommy Dennis was a great showman. In the weeks leading up to Christmas the front of the shop groaned under the weight of turkeys, pheasants, chickens and hares. The sign over the shop front was repainted annually in red, green and gold as also were the vans. Tommy himself was always extremely smart, dressed in the nattiest of suitings. He became very popular as a parish councillor and prominent in the British Legion. He had that happy knack of knowing everyone in Ashwell and district whether customer or not and had a cheery word for everyone passing the shop. When a customer's husband, wife or children were in Addenbrooke's Hospital, Cambridge, Tommy volunteered to convey the relatives on visiting days.

Somewhat before my time Thomas Flitton, a working miller, had rented the Fordham mill at the bottom of Mill Street. When I first remember him, he lived in the house, originally the court house of the Manor of Westbury Nernewtes (now wrongly called Digswell manor). It stands just to the west of Ashwell Stores and part of the rear buildings was a malting until the middle of the nineteenth century. These premises Tommy Flitton used as a cycle shop; he was an agent for Rudge Whitworth cycles, and even when very old with trembling hands, he still did cycle repairs and hired out cycles for a few pence a day.

Bacons Yard, the little housing development, keeps alive the name of an old Ashwell family of churchwardens, farmers, harness and ropemakers, who had lived in Ashwell for a very long time. The last of the Bacons, Billy sold the saddlery with the house and yard in 1895 and retired to the Red House, now known as Townsend Close, in Lucas Lane.

Mrs Wolverley Fordham was anxious to set up a model dairy and at the same time retain the harness-makers business. There were at least a score of horses on her farms. The tall thatched barn was converted into a milking parlour with a set of new buildings behind, where the milk was cooled and some separated to produce cream, the skimmed milk afterwards being fed to the calves. Part of the yard was fenced off to form a sort of assembly point where the cows waited patiently to be taken twice daily into the parlour to be milked by hand.

The long rope walk, where Mr Bacon's employees had walked backwards twirling their rope-making swivels, became the walk of the cows to pastures new, and the Bacon's house was occupied by the head cowman. Mr Lewis and Mr Sam Radford carried on as though nothing had happened, sitting behind the same benches, stitching away with their waxed thread in mending the harness of probably a hundred Ashwell farm carthorses, plus all those from Doctor Woodforde's empire, and in addition, near harvest time, patching and re-battening the tough canvasses used on the Massey Harris self binders, from the same farms. This shop, now known as the Old Saddlery, had its own peculiar smells of leather and canvas, saddle soap and wax.

A large glass wall case contained a good selection of the necessary equipment used with horses, whips, genuine horse brasses, little brass bells which were fixed to the top of the horses' halters, ear protectors with tassels to shake off flies in hot weather. Rolls of coarse red, white or blue cotton ribbon which proud horsemen plaited into the horses' tails and manes were also available; tins of saddle soap, neatsfoot oil, bottles of Ellimans embrocation, tins of Brasso, dubbin and Cherry Blossom boot polish, leather leggings, canvas leggings and boot laces. There were also leather reins and dog collars, thin rope reins and long cart ropes used to tie on the load of sheaves during harvest time, hurricane lamps, pretty glass and china lamps, brass lamps, spare lamp glasses and wicks and packets of Prices candles.

Unlike a certain other West End, Ashwell's was not a shopping centre, although John Worboys' tiny shop, now converted into a garage, at the west end of Back Street, was packed from floor to ceiling with almost everything the housewife of those days needed. There was always a side of bacon from which the rashers were cut by hand, a whole red cheese and penny blocks of salt the size of a brick, packets of red Lifebuoy and yellow Sunlight soap. John, always known as Jack, had a bad leg and apart from the shop he was Ashwell's official town crier and bill sticker, as was his father before him. Organisers of parish meetings, whist drives, concerts, circuses, sales of crockery on Carter's pond, sales of timber in the Three Tuns yard and jumble sales - for all of these and many more, Jack would paste up the notices, ring his bell and make the announcements in several parts of the village. The town crier's bell now rests in Ashwell museum, and his shop was taken over by Byron Searle's mother for a time.

Number 7 Swan Street was another of these tiny general shops, which stocked a little of everything. It had been in Julia Garrett's family for a good many years. My father once told me that as a schoolboy he went there to buy a ha'porth of bulls eyes and dipped his fingers, as he thought, into a barrel of sugar, but on tasting found it was silver sand, which in those days was often sprinkled on a floor before sweeping! The next owner of the shop, Miss Kitty Goss, brought it into the twentieth century, although some twenty years late. An enamelled sign below the small shop window announced Brooke Bonds tea and along the front of the counter a row of biscuit tins with glass lids displayed samples of Macfarlane Langs and Carrs of Carlisle biscuits. On the shelves behind, glass jars with the name of Garratt & Cannon, Confectioners of Hitchin, contained such delights as gob stoppers, vinegar pats, butter pats, bulls eyes and pear drops.

Boxes of bars of Caleys chocolate, packets of Barretts sherbert dabs, sherbert fountains, sweet tobacco, sweet cigarettes and liquorice boot laces sold at a halfpenny or penny apiece, and Miss Goss' special line, newly introduced from the United States, Wrigleys Juicy Fruit chewing gum. Soon Miss Goss became known as Miss Juicy Fruit.

Opposite the lych gate in Mill Street was the Butcher's shop of Arthur Bryant, with Mrs Bryant, sons Kenneth and Mortimer and daughter Margery. I can remember only the strings of sausages, enamel bowls of dripping and brawn and glazed red earthenware pots of salted meat. In 1920, after the tragic suicide of Arthur Bryant, the shop was bought by Mark Victor Crump, a smart young butcher, also an ex-Service man. He brought up-to-date standards of hygiene to the old shop and premises and at the same time raised a family of four sons. Two of his grandsons carry on the business today.

Thousands of boys from the Merchant Taylors' School must have watched the slaughter of bullocks by poleaxe and pigs and sheep by the knife at the slaughterhouse in Workhouse Yard. If my memory is correct, bullocks were slaughtered on Mondays. As we came out of school at noon, it was a mad rush to get the best view over the half door of the slaughterhouse. Sometimes, if the poleaxe missed the vital spot, the animal would go down only to rise again in an attempt to escape. I can still hear the blood-curdling screams of pigs being killed. Afterwards, the pig was put in a large wooden tub of hot water and the bristles scraped off with a scud, a metal tool shaped like a sink plunger. After this treatment, the flesh looked so nice and clean, much better than lamb's or bullock's, which is probably why I prefer pork.

This Butcher's shop had its window blinds lowered more than any other in Ashwell, but not because it was closed for business. From very early times (probably Elizabethan, when many death customs originated) until about the end of the 1930s, it was the custom on the day of a funeral for blinds to be drawn along the route of the funeral procession, as a mark of respect to the dead person and the relatives. Thus the butcher would lower the blinds before the hand-drawn bier or later the motor driven hearse arrived at the lych gate for the service in Church.

One shop I had forgotten. In that little triangle at the junction of West End and Back Street were a thatched cottage, a slate roof cottage and a third, also thatched, but condemned by the Local Authority. This last, long since pulled down, was the Fish and Chip shop. The three cottages had housed employees of Joshua Page, the brewer, who I believe owned the cottages and lived at the brewery house opposite (now Westbury House) until about 1920 when the brewery closed, and its public houses were taken over by the Biggleswade brewers, Wells and Winch. At that time - and indeed until well after the second world war - there was a box for posting letters built into the Westbury House garden wall. For a short cut for the people of Back Street to post their letters, Mr Page made a footpath known as the Twitchell, which at the same time gave his family and maids quicker access to Jack Worboys' general shop in Back Street. In the early 1920s two young men brought a take-away to Ashwell. Fred Harris and "Curly" from either Henlow or Arlesey opened a shop in the condemned thatched cottage where a piece of fried fish could be bought for twopence and a generous portion of chips for one penny, wrapped in newspaper - no such refinements as grease-proof in those days. After a time it was realised that the coal-fired fish pans were a fire hazard under a thatched roof, so the shop was moved into a building near the Engine public house in Back Street.

This railway engine at Hitchin stationyard in 1866 had left the rails two miles from Ashwell Station, ending in a field of barley. The driver and fireman were killed.
(T.B. Latchmore)

The Ashwell Taxi Service, c.1920.
Charles Reynolds with his horse and fly. On the right Mrs Reynolds and her father in law Mynot Reynolds. The building was behind the Springs Cottages recently renovated.
(Museum)

The Fordham horses, early 1900s, before steam and petrol power.
(Museum)

One of the earliest Foden Steamers in close-up. Note: Speed 5 m.p.h. Year 1912.
(Museum)

Fordham's Brewery, 1932. The fleet of lorries and drivers from left to right: John Davies, Edward Wilkins, Ernest Kingsley (Transport Manager), Sidney Sheldrick, Snowy Reynolds, Herbert Skerman, Benjamin Seeby.
(Town & Country News, 1932)

The Foden Steamers, with Mr Ernest Kingsley, late 1920s.
(Town & Country News, 1932)

Top left: *Ashwell's first car – a De Dion Bouton, owned by Dr R.E.H. Woodforde, seen driving out with his wife, in the early 1900s. He sold it in 1914 in part exchange for a new Ford for £30 and retaining the headlamps!* (Oliver Woodforde)

Top right: *Edward Snow Fordham (1858-1919) of Elbrook House, London Stipendiary Magistrate and owner of the Napier below. The Vanity Fair magazine published this "Spy" cartoon of him.* (Museum)

Left: *Running repairs in 1930.*

Below: *Edward Snow Fordham's Napier car – specially strengthened to take his weight!* (Museum)

THE 6-CYLINDER "NAPIER."

A contrast in styles.
Above: *Neville Howes, (c.1925), setting off with his horse and float and two boys to deliver the milk. Note the Grange Dovehouse, still recognisable, but now converted for human habitation.*
(Mr & Mrs P. Howes)

Below: *He enjoyed a rather more tranquil existence with his electric van – c.1938.*
(Mr & Mrs P. Howes)

A MURPHY 8-10 CWT. DAIRY PRODUCE DISTRIBUTION VAN IN RURAL HERTFORDSHIRE.

Enterprising Interlopers

If you thought the inhabitants of Ashwell were well catered for with the variety of shops and other businesses I have mentioned, you would be quite wrong, at least several outsiders thought so. Messrs W.B. Moss and Sons, high class provision merchants, specialists in "first crop tea", furnishers, etc, with their headquarters at Hitchin and branches in several other towns, sent their Mr Duffield from the Baldock branch on his bicycle through Bygrave, Ashwell and Newnham collecting orders which would be delivered later in the week.

Another of these interlopers was Bernard. Wearing a white jacket and apron with fringes at the bottom, he drove his horse and van from Dunton every Saturday. The van was specially built to accommodate a small stock of provisions, tin kettles, brushes and pans, and he seemed to do all his business at the west end of Ashwell and usually turned the van round between 7 and 8 p.m. for the return journey to Dunton.

The other end of the village was catered for by Mr Gulliver who wore one of those khaki warehouse coats. A leather money bag hung by a strap over his shoulder, and well polished leggings and boots showed below the coat. He came from Steeple Morden with a van very much like Bernard's and in addition to some provisions sold vinegar by the pint from a wooden barrel, candles, matches, and pots and pans, which rattled as the van wheels negotiated the potholes in the granite and mud roads of those days. He also sold paraffin oil from a large flat tank slung beneath the van.

Driving a pony and trap, Mr Bob Kitchener (a very fat man) came over from Hinxworth to sell bread several times a week.

"Kipper Yarmer" (Yarmouth) was a familiar street cry on Monday and Friday mornings. It heralded the approach of "Frenchie" from Wrens', the Biggleswade fishmongers. Their horse-drawn vehicle loaded with boxes of winkles, herrings, kippers, bloaters, cod and sprats was protected from the elements by a piece of old tarpaulin. Some of the regular customers would meet "Frenchie" at West End in order to buy the freshest of the fish after the seven-mile journey from Biggleswade. After stops at the Engine and the Rose and Crown, he would wend his fishy way to the Bushel and Strike, by which time most of the smelly boxes were empty.

For some years a butcher found it worthwhile to drive his van load of meat the seven miles from Royston to Ashwell, in spite of the fact that there were already three established butchers. Tommy Danes, wearing a blue and white striped apron over his khaki warehouse coat, would announce his arrival with a flourish of his knife and sharpening steel.

Then there were the Misses Harper from Guilden Morden bakery, with quite a lot of Ashwell customers. In those days there was very little choice of bread. You either had a cottage loaf, a large or small tinned loaf or, if you were one of the peculiar people, you bought the then new-fangled Hovis brown bread.

Except for bank holidays, every Monday morning Mr Hibbert left his home at Arlesey and following a regular route of footpaths and bridleways arrived at Ashwell just before nine o'clock carrying a bundle of brass-ended rods and his sweep's brush on his shoulder. His little flat cap, his clothes and even his boots were impregnated with soot, and for sixpence a chimney, he worked his way through the village. As well as the rods and brush, he carried a hammer and nails to fix his piece of sooty sacking over the fireplace of the chimney to be swept. Soon after five in the evening the agile little man would be seen striding along "Carcot hedge", the bridleway leading to Caldecote, Stotfold, and back home to Arlesey.

Ashwell did have a resident sweep in those days, John Waldock, known as "Johnny Civil" or "Civil Johnny", a pleasant little man who lived in the brick built cottage (owned at that time by Mr Bacon) which had been built behind "the Cottage" next to the Cricketers. I rather think most of his chimney sweeping was in that part of the village.

I have read that towards the end of the last century, the big London shops allowed their customers a year's grace before sending out bills. According to a certain lady, writing in the "Fortnightly Review" of January 1895, "We bought our goods and dutifully followed in the footsteps of our forefathers, paying for the goods at the end of the year, for no well-thought-of firm ever demanded or expected more than a yearly payment of debts". It is very doubtful whether the Ashwell shopkeepers could afford to do this. In the 1920s they supplied each of their better-off customers with order books. These were made up monthly and accounts sent out accordingly. The travelling salesmen - Bernard, Mr Gulliver, Frenchie and the others - could not run their business in this way. With them it was strictly cash down.

I have left two men until last because they were the originators of "never-never", hire purchase or plastic money. Dapper Mr Armstrong, Scottish, bowler-hatted, wearing a well cut tailor-made suit and grey spats over highly polished shoes, drove over from Bedford once weekly in a smart Ford car. Mr Armstrong was a "tally man". He supplied readymade clothing to a number of regular customers, collecting the money in weekly instalments. Actually he preferred the made-to-measure business: it was higher class and probably higher profits. The Rose and Crown was his chief drinking house, and he was quite often seen running his tape measure over a customer in the pub yard - the ceilings were too low and it was too dark to do the measuring inside. The other tally man, Mr Harris, who I understand came from Hitchin, was quite the opposite in his cloth cap, Norfolk jacket, breeches and leggings. Mr Harris's transport was a horse and trap and his customers were not quite so upmarket.

Larks, Gourmets and declining customs

In the twenties, long before the days of poisonous crop spraying, the song of the lark was so common that we thought nothing of it, until it was too late. Even before the crop sprayers, there were mass killers of larks. During winter as the snow lay crisp and even, out came the lark catchers. The equipment was simple. A length of white string twenty or thirty yards long, each end fastened to a wooden reel on which the string was very carefully wound - carefully because every few inches was attached a white horse hair snare. The line was pegged down low across a field, each snare opened large enough for a lark to thrust its head. Then raisins soaked in whisky or brandy were scattered as bait near the line.

Early in the morning, the catchers collected the larks, often frozen solid in the little horse-hair snares. London's best hotels served these as a very expensive delicacy, and several London buyers supplied the catchers with special labels for the bundles of larks to be despatched as early as possible by passenger train from Ashwell station.

Catching sparrows in bulk needed a length of fairly small mesh netting tied between two light poles, usually hazel, eight or ten feet long. After dark, when the sparrows had settled for the night under the eaves of thatched cottage roofs or of corn stacks, the two sparrow catchers set out, sweeping along the eaves trapping the sleepy birds in their nets - ready for the next day's sparrow pie.

If you had imagined that the French were the only people to eat snails you would be wrong. Some Ashwell folk were eating them from at least the beginning of the century and probably before that. Joe Man was well known in certain circles for his snail suppers. The snails were at their best and sweetest when, during the winter, they had gone into hibernation and the shell opening was sealed over. They were found glued to walls and fences. Joe reckoned that the fattest and most succulent were to be found attached to the walls of outside privies in the gardens where he lived by the Springs. When the time was ripe, Joe would invite his friends to the grand supper. The Ashwell "escargots" would be lightly boiled and served with bread, butter, pepper and salt.

The main rookery was for many years in the little Back Lane behind the Merchant Taylors' School orchard and in front of the Bury park. Then for some reason the birds left. From time to time there were rook shoots to reduce numbers. Some people were fond of rook pie. In the grounds of a large house near Ashwell, I once saw a large cage about eight feet square. Some kind of bait lured the rooks through a trap door and each day a man with a heavy stick entered the cage to beat the rooks to death.

Pigeons have been a source of food for over a thousand years in many countries. Ashwell church tower was their home after the "dovehouse" at the rectory fell down early this century. The birds moved into the builders' scaffold holes and nested there until 1928, when the tower was repaired and those holes were filled in.

The Rector, the Rev S.W.P. Webb, collected the eggs and gave them to poor people. A well-known saying of his to children was "Would you like a threepenny bit or a pigeon's egg?"

The little Rector was quite a good shot. He had a leather holster fixed to the front forks of his bicycle in which he thrust a double-barrelled gun. At harvest time he would cycle with his gun out to the field of one of his flock, usually John Sale or Ben Christy, and settle himself down on a few sheaves of corn at one corner of the field. As the horse-drawn Massey Harris self-binder drew near, he took aim hoping that the noise would frighten a hare, rabbit, partridge or, if he was very lucky, a pheasant into his sights. Pheasants were rather rare, whereas the red-legged or French partridge and the ordinary partridge were quite common. Usually the scared creatures crept further into the corn, and waited until only a few square yards remained, then, rather than be cut down by the binder's blades, made a dash for freedom.

I was told a poacher's story concerning an Ashwell man named Mole, who on an autumn evening was caught poaching by a certain farmer. After confiscating the gun, the farmer remarked, "You have got the wrong name, it should be fox!"

In the twenties the horse-drawn Massey Harris self-binder and collecting the sheaves by hand usually left a quantity of wheat or barley on the ground. As soon as all the sheaves of corn had been cleared from a field, the gleaners were allowed in, to pick up the surplus, unless one shock of corn was left standing near the entrance to the field. This indicated that either the field had not been dragged by a horse-drawn rake or the farmer did not want people on his land.

Gleaning was a very old custom and part of village life. During the gleaning season, the gleaners' bell was rung from the church tower at 9 a.m. and at 5 p.m. Woe betide anyone caught gleaning before or after those times! Although the gleaners' bell was discontinued during the war, gleaning was more than ever necessary, not only to feed the chickens, but also for grain to be ground into flour to supplement wartime rations. The women gleaners wore a sacking apron turned up to form a sort of envelope, leaving both hands free to pick up the ears of corn. Children wore a bag made out of an old sheet tied round their waist, also leaving both hands free.

The keeping of backyard chickens declined as we went into the 1940s and so the gleaner died out.

Moles and polecats were apparently a nuisance in the 18th and early 19th centuries. The churchwardens' account books record payments for large numbers of these creatures. In the 1920s rats and rabbits were a great nuisance, consuming great quantities of grain. Some farmers paid rat catchers so much per dozen for dead rats. I remember a large boarded barn near Ashwell End house, where scores of rats' tails were nailed to the tarred boards for everyone to see.

Colonies of rabbits were to be found at the Hinxworth road quarries, the Lime Kiln Lane quarries and the sandpits on Kingsland Road, and no doubt many other places, all conveniently situated near growing crops. Ferreting the rabbits was a winter Saturday afternoon's sport for a number of Ashwell men, with the blessing of the farmer. The rabbits could be sold for at least sixpence each. The buyer would carefully skin the animal, carefully because when Mr Loveridge from Biggleswade came round, he would stretch out the skin. If it was torn, he would not pay as much as for a perfect one. It was just the same with the little mole skins.

Ashwell has always had thatched roofs, mainly because straw was a local product and cheaper to use than imported Bedfordshire clay tiles or Welsh slates. Each farm had its own thatcher who undertook the thatching of hay, corn and straw stacks, but whereas stack thatching was required to last only for a few months until thrashing time, the job of thatching a house or barn had to be done by an expert. It would last for a good many years. But Ashwell, with its variety of tradesmen, did not have a single house thatcher - the bowler-hatted Hummerston brothers from Wrestlingworth were always called in to do the thatching.

Men of the Roads

Until the twenties, the village's roads were composed of broken granite, which was pressed into the surface by water and a steam roller. Herts County Council's Ashwell team consisted of Charles Gallant, Fred Pettengell, Charles Worboys (known as Charley Foreman) and James Worboys (not related to Charles). The last named, known as Jimmy Tight, unfortunately had a huge pitted strawberry nose. Each roadman was obliged to wear a large brass plate, bearing his number and the letters

H.C.C., strapped to his right leg just below the knee. Any person who spotted a roadman leaning on his broom, or leaving his job before time could report him to Mr William Cooper or any other county councillor.

The team did a good job, keeping the roads swept in several villages for the weekly wage of 28 shillings, against the 30 shillings they might have earned on a farm at that time. When tarmac first came to Ashwell, the road gang was kept busy. The tar was heated in a large circular boiler, then drawn off by means of a tap into a large watering can. The hot tar was then sprinkled thickly, but evenly, on to the old granite road surface, then a layer of a greyish sort of sand was spread over the tar, which left a sticky mess for several days, until the tar had completely set. This tarring could only be carried out when the road surface was dry. It was a slow job and it was a few years before all Ashwell's roads were treated. Kerbed footpaths were unknown until the 1930s.

Fred Pettengell's wife, Adelaide, a staunch member of the Women's Institute, invented a special kind of knitted combined collar and neck-tie for men. The collar was knitted in white wool and the attached tie in pale blue. It must be remembered that men's shirts were then without collars. Collars were bought separately and attached by back and front studs; so most working men wore a neckerchief, or a collar and tie when they put on their Sunday best suit.

Adelaide Pettingell's father was always known as Joe Man - his real name was Herbert George Worboys. Joe (or Herbert) was well known for his straw plait. All the big houses in Ashwell had one of Joe's corn dollies hanging in the hall. This skill Joe passed on to his grandson Percy Pettengell, which Percy developed in the form of various models including ploughs and Ashwell church.

Ashwell had its share of gipsies, the genuine gipsies - the Smiths and Loveridges - who lived in crude tents, washed in the streams, made and sold clothes pegs and paper flowers, and pushed a knife and scissor grinder round the village streets.

Their most popular haunt in the twenties was at Paddocks, that little strip of land in the hollow - a sort of no-man's-land which divides Steeple Morden from Ashwell with the stream also forming the boundary between Hertfordshire and Cambridgeshire. Here were also the sheep-dipping troughs, which I suppose belonged to the parish.

Sheltered from the cold winds by trees and bushes on each side, it was an ideal spot for the gipsies to camp, with water from the stream, rabbits, hares and partridges in the nearby fields, and vegetables stolen from the Paddocks' allotments close by. The other gipsy haunts were at Whitegates, at the boundary between Ashwell and Eyeworth, and at a few points along Ruddery, and Ashwell Street. The parents of the great evangelist, Gipsy Smith, were often in the Ashwell area.

Lousy Bush, an ancient hawthorn tree stood as a sort of boundary marker for three parishes - Ashwell, Newnham and Caldecote. It was also a gipsy site. The strange pieces of cloth which often hung from the branches were said to be gipsy prayer rags. Its ivy-clad trunk was split through age and pitted with woodworm escape holes. It was blown down in the 1930s.

Laying the sewers in Spring Head in the early 1900s. Ashwell people know what digging up roads is all about!!
(Mrs B. Wallace)

One of Henry Bowman's 1908 Postcards, illustrating Mill Street and his house, Waterfall and Vinery, Chapel Lawn and Summer House. Note the intricate decoration of the latter, now a barn used for Badminton.
(Museum)

The Recreation Ground, c.1900
A place where sheep could safely graze.
(Museum)

Wonderful photograph (c.1930) showing the chalk formation of Walkden's Clunch pits, near Ashwell Street, now owned by Hugh Jarman. (G. Shelton)

The Mill & Mill House, c.1920. Below the Dove nesting boxes is the sign of Aston Ayres, an engineer and Motor Mechanic, who later introduced the Cinema to Ashwell Village Hall. Later he built new Cinemas at Baldock and Stevenage. (D. Shelton)

Left: *Cattle sheds near Bluegates Dairy, now Bacon's Yard Development in the High Street.* (Philip Coverdale)

Below: *A very familiar sight before 1939. Driving the horse and cart is probably Ernie Webb, whose widow is now the oldest inhabitant of Ashwell – 98 in 1991. (Museum)*

Dixies Farm and Bear Farm barns, now redeveloped. Note the white block is the remains of a cob wall. (Philip Coverdale)

Above: *Claybush trees, c.1920.*
The two elm trees were a landmark, seen for miles around. Now sadly only the stumps remain. Note the thatched corn stack.
(Museum)

Left: *The Windmill and Engine Shed at Ashwell Water Works, Bygrave Road – regrettably demolished in the 1950s.*
(Frank Sheldrick)

This photograph of the unique cob wall was taken shortly after it had been re-thatched in 1972. While the photograph is outside our period, the wall was built about 1900 by among others John Sheldrick, the author's grandfather. (Philip Coverdale)

Delivering Fordham's Ale to "The Stone Jug" at Clophill, Beds. c.1925. Pictured are the publican and the engine driver, Bill Harvey. (The author)

Right: *A remarkable photograph of the exposed timberwork of the Forresters Cottages prior to restoration. The cottages had narrowly escaped demolition in 1962. The lady in the foreground was Mrs E. Gray, wife of Mrs W.A. Fordham's chauffeur.* (Museum)

Below: *The Adelong – built in 1881 by W.P. Edwards, who found gold in Adelong, Australia. He brought back a white cockatoo, which lived on into the 1930s, and a collection of Australian minerals which his sister later gave to Ashwell Museum.* (Museum)
Below right: *Silas Worboys' Wheelwright Workshop: demolished in 1975 when in a dangerous condition.* (Philip Coverdale)

Of Church, Chapel and Sunday Newspapers

"Six days shalt thou labour" was still the maxim at Ashwell in the early twenties. On the farms, the horsekeepers and stockmen only fed and watered their charges on Sundays. Allotments and gardens were out of bounds; children went to morning and afternoon Sunday school. Many nonconformist families would not allow a Sunday newspaper in the house; in fact, I knew one man who lived with his daughter and family and had his newspaper delivered to a neighbour, then smuggled it into his room. Others would not allow their children to ride bicycles on Sunday. A Sunday school friend of mine told me that his father forgot to bring in a cabbage for the Sunday meal. On Sunday, while father was at church, mother cut a cabbage, but father refused to eat it!

A & C Christy, the newsagents, put up the shutters on Saturday evening. Sunday newspapers could be bought in Ashwell only by ordering from William White, who lived in one of the Back Street Foresters cottages, and he or one of his sons would deliver to your door on Sunday mornings. Bill White worked as an estate carpenter at Ducklake farm, repaired gates, fences and other woodwork around the farm. The professional carpenter/joiner, who actually made doors and staircases and all the necessary woodwork for houses, looked down on the estate carpenter and described him as a "hedgerow carpenter".

If you were not too choosy about your Sunday reading and the "News of the World" would satisfy you, it was necessary to order it from George Revels, who seemed to have the sole rights to that newspaper. George lived in one of the council houses on Beacon Leg Hill, pronounced "Bacon Leg" by Ashwellians. In earlier days he was known as chemist Revels (pronounced chimmist) because in his youth he had worked for the chemist in High Street who had made rat poisons and veterinary products.

I would often cycle the seven miles to visit cousins in Letchworth on a Sunday morning and, in spite of there being a dozen or more religious sects in the garden city, I would see men putting up fences and digging their allotments and gardens. They put on their best clothes in the afternoon and went along to the Cloisters, where you could buy sweets and icecreams and listen to the band.

The Rev John Bailey, then vicar of Norton, nearby, told me that when invited to preach at Ashwell church he afterwards went to the rectory - a straggling house of long dark passages, lit by oil lamps and candles, partly overgrown with ivy and surrounded by trees - and felt he was stepping back into the days of Charles Dickens. I remember one Sunday morning in 1925 as we choirboys searched for bats among the worn and musty cassocks before preparing for the morning service, Mr William Cooper, churchwarden, county councillor and gentleman, with ample waist and gold watch chain suspended in two loops across it, hands clasped behind his back beneath his coat tails - it might have been Mr Pickwick - entered the vestry and said quite simply, "The rector has died, there will be no morning service". After 33 years as rector of the Church of St Mary the Virgin, Samuel William Panajotti Webb had passed on.

Very soon there blew a wind of change, strangely enough from South Africa. The Bishop of St. Albans, the Rt. Rev. Michael Furse, inducted into the living the Rev. Henry A Griffith, an old friend who had served with him in South Africa. Before it could be occupied, almost half of the rectory was pulled down and the remainder modernised. The new rector had also been a chaplain to H.M. Forces during the Great War and had seen men dig and die in the trenches in Flanders. So when I paid a visit to borrow some early church records one Sunday afternoon, I was not at all surprised to find him among the sweet peas with his shirt sleeves rolled up. He also had a Sunday newspaper delivered to the rectory.

John Picking of the old carpenter family was sexton and bell-chimer through most of the long reign of the Rev. S.W.P. Webb, whilst Herbert Pack, an employee of Fordham's brewery, was leading choirman and in charge of the church clock. In those days, it was a lengthy business winding up the two heavy clock weights by hand twice weekly up in the bell ringers' chamber.

During the twenties, the parish church, dedicated to St Mary the Virgin, was a rather dull building smelling of damp and paraffin oil. The central heating was not very efficient and at some time in the past the chancel windows had been painted white and the large east window, which until the reign of Henry VIII depicted the martyrdom of Thomas a-Becket, was partly blacked out by a large dark felt or canvas screen, whilst the floor was paved with red and blue quarry tiles as used in small pubs and beerhouses.

Although the pews in Ashwell church were not numbered 1st, 2nd and 3rd class as were the railway carriages, the best pews were occupied by the village gentry, who paid for the privilege. Reginald Hine, who lived at Ashwell for a time, describes the morning service in his book, "Confessions of an Uncommon Attorney":

"The Rector bore the name of the Rev. Panajotti Webb, and he, too, was something of an eccentric. He would so choose his text and manipulate his sermon as to illustrate the besetting sins of leading members of his congregation. There was no need for him to name those against whom his words were pointed. We almost cheered as the shafts went home. In those days the nave pews were occupied in descending degrees of social importance. It was right therefore that the squire or his lady should be shown up first. Then came the turn of the rector's warden, who sat behind him. For services rendered, he was let off lightly. Not so the people's warden, who often felt it his duty to oppose, and even thwart, the rector. When he had been faithfully dealt with, the tenant farmers were made to squirm and tremble in their seats. Woe betide them if they happened to be behind with their tithes! Next in order of attack were the nondescript residents like myself, who afforded plenty of opportunities for sly innuendo or direct animadversion. And finally the rector would upbraid and castigate the shopkeepers, who appeared capable of all manner of wickedness.

So, after a long and trying sermon, we would stagger out of church of a Sunday morning, all of us miserable sinners, but each comforted by the thought that he was not much worse than the others, and that the rector himself, if he only knew it, was not without besetting sins of his own."

The Rev. Samuel Panajotti Webb with his wife Hattie came to the living in 1892. There were no little Webbs, but Mrs Webb ran a school for well-to-do young ladies. The Webbs employed a gardener, two maids and several part-time helpers to look after the over-large rectory. Apart from being small in stature, the rector was extremely low church, and so after his death the parishioners were in for a shock.

The new rector, the Rev. Henry Allday Griffith, and Margaret, his wife, were also childless. For some time they were in rooms with Mrs Parkhouse at Woodlands in High

Street, whilst the rectory was cut down in size and modernised. Whilst this was going on, an appeal was launched to raise a considerable sum of money to repair the crumbling church tower. The tower was encased in scaffolding and repaired during 1928 and 1929, followed by a number of alterations to the interior. The roof timbers were cobwebbed, the walls cleaned and limewashed, the 17th century oak communion table was moved into the Lady Chapel together with the Victorian brass, altar cross, candlesticks and vases, and at the high altar a new table had not only an oak cross and candlesticks, but a coloured altar cloth.

When the new rector wore vestments for the sacraments there was much shaking of heads and it was whispered that the church was going Roman. But, history really does repeat itself, for when in the 1860s the rood screen was thrown out, the Lady chapel dismantled with its two oak screens used to form a choir vestry and a storeplace and the east window blacked out, churchwarden Bacon of the saddlery in High Street wrote in his account book cum diary: "April 1868. Church altered - all the old seats taken out - organ brought here about 3rd April and Sunday the 5th the 16 singers appeared in white, as some say with their shirts outside. The alterations are generally complained of as ritualistic and gradually approaching Roman Catholicism - a crisis is about happening."

The faithful soon settled down to the new order, as no doubt their forefathers did in 1868, and the new rector became very popular with his parishioners of all denominations. In fact one Catholic lady who was not able to attend the church at Baldock became a regular communicant. However, a frustrated spinster, Miss Huggins, known locally as Deaconess Dora, made life a little difficult for him, and in 1934 he accepted the Dunstable living where he became a Canon.

His place was taken by the Rev. F.H.J. Newton, who left the townspeople of Blackheath to convert the country folk of Ashwell. He had an angelic face and a twinkle in his eye, smoked his cigarettes in a holder and drove a noisy fast car, but when he entered the Chancel door he became a different man, his shoes were replaced by soft soled black leather shoes adorned with large silver buckles. For a time it was feared that the normal Holy Communion services would be discontinued when the 9a.m. Sung Eucharist was introduced with the Rector's own specially printed service books. A high churchman, he liked to be known as Father Newton, not at all to the liking of those who favoured Panajotti Webb's thinking. The makers of Bovril awarded the Rector a cash prize for his slogan 'BOVRIL PUTS BEEF INTO YOU' but it soon became evident that he preferred beer to Bovril when casks of Fordham's beer were delivered to the Rectory and he would often pop into the Three Tuns with a case containing two quart bottles to be filled with Simpson's beer.

Toward the end of a funeral service in church one afternoon the Rector gave the usual signal to the undertaker, Fred Bray, and the coffin was carried out of the church, followed by the mourners, when suddenly the Rector halted and said to Fred Bray, "I have forgotten the two hymns". But Fred replied, "Just carry on, we can't go back now".

Mrs Newton ran a school for young ladies. When invited to preside over the Mothers' Union she replied, "Like the Holy Ghost, I shall look on".

A little group including Robert Christy, Eric Harradine, John Bray, Wilfred Barrow and I formed a Toc H branch in Ashwell. We paid a peppercorn rent to Mrs Fordham for the use of the old Pages Brewery stables and met weekly to discuss all kinds of topics. One night I explained what life was like in the workhouse. I had visited an old school teacher at Royston workhouse and worked for six months building an extension to the Cambridge workhouse. At Christmas the group formed a mixed choir to sing carols round the village. We collected so much money that we were able to take parcels of slippers, sweets and oranges to the Ashwell inmates of both Royston and Hitchin workhouses and Days baked 50 fruit cakes which we delivered on Christmas Eve to widows and old Ashwell folk. The Toc H carol singers sang on well into the war years.

The Rev James Edgar Chew, a bachelor with a domineering mother, became Rector in1938 for three years.

Church people patronised the grocer, J.H. Christy and Son, because the Christys were church, whereas the Congregationalists took their trade to Westropes, who were members of that chapel. The minister from 1919 was the Rev. A.M. Perkins, a learned man and keen astronomer who, with his wife and daughter, lived at the manse in Kingsland Way. The chapel, well set back from High Street, is one of Ashwell's nicer looking buildings.

Mr J.W. Bailey, the builder, and his wife were among the chapel's main supporters. Apart from their trip to the United States on the maiden voyage of the Queen Mary, they went out regularly to the Swiss ski slopes, when only the wealthy did that sort of thing. There were frequent visits to Paris, where Mrs Bailey was able to purchase the latest creations. The people of Ashwell could be given a preview of what the best dressed ladies of Paris would be wearing when she set off each Sunday morning at precisely 10.55 to walk from her home at Westbury House, arriving at the chapel gates as the church clock struck 11, and then in the final parade up the chapel aisle the congregation could admire her fine Paris hats and frocks.

From about 1861 to 1900 there had been a Primitive Methodist chapel at West End, now turned into two cottages. My father remembered attending a service here at which the great preacher Gipsy Smith preached.

The following incident is revealing. Ebenezer Saunderson, miller and coal merchant of Steeple Morden, supplied householders of the district with a large ex-army truck driven by Charles Potton and Walter Hitch, both well known in Steeple Morden. Charles Potton was the only man in the district to have made front page news in the periodical "John Bull".

I knew him quite well. If my memory is correct, when a young member of the Steeple Morden Wesleyan chapel in the early 1900s, he obtained work with the Vicar of Steeple Morden, whereupon the Vicar ordered Charles to attend church services. He refused and was sacked. "John Bull" publicised the case.

Above: *The unique graffiti on the tower wall. Translated: '1000, 3 times 100, 5 × 10. A pitiable, fierce, violent (plague departed), a wretched populace survives to witness ... And in the end a mighty wind Maurus thunders in this year in the world 1361'.* (Museum)

Left: *A copy of Miss Charlotte Morice's drawing of the Parish Church and Lych Gate in 1840, by M.T. Woodforde.* (O. Woodforde)

Below: *Ashwell Church from the Rectory garden. Note the thatched Summer House. The photograph is pre-1928, when the tower was repaired. Also note the builder's original scaffold pudloc holes where pigeons nested.* (Museum)

The Parish Church Choir before 1914 – men and boys.
Note Mr Chote the Headmaster on extreme left, with Rev Panajotti Webb on his right.
(Author)

Ashwell Church interior, c.1920.
Electric lighting was paid for by Sir William Gentle c.1931 and the old oil lamps removed.
Note the pulpit on the right of chancel arch and the copper memorial above it to the memory of William Cooper's son who was killed in the Boer War.
(Museum)

The Strict Baptist Chapel in Gardiners Lane was built in 1852 by Mr Flitton (a miller) in the garden of his house now Little Garth in Mill Street. Now called Zoar Baptist Chapel. (Northern family)

The Wesleyan Methodust Chapel, c.1950. The iron railings were taken away during World War II. The Chapel was built in 1880 to replace a smaller one in Church Lane. The 1880 Chapel was pulled down in 1979. (Museum)

The Congregational Church in 1910. Now known as the United Reformed Church. (Peter Greener)

Ye Olde Tin Can ...

The village owes its first bus service to a London hat manufacturer. Cockney Henry Leverett, wearing a cloth cap and neckerchief, bought the strange white house on Ashwell Street at the top of Bear Lane, which has been used as a factory of various kinds for some years now. I believe it was built as a retirement home for Fred Bailey, founder of the Ashwell firm of F.J. Bailey & Co., Builders, timber merchants, lime burners and undertakers.

When Henry Leverett moved in, in the late twenties, there were the usual village rumours. Something mysterious was going on; two fierce chow dogs patrolled the house and grounds day and night. But after a time, Henry made himself known to the regulars at the Rose & Crown and following a few rounds of drinks, he didn't seem a bad sort of chap; in fact he made it known that he was building a bus! In due course, the strange vehicle emerged - a mixture of polished aluminium and red paint. A sign above the windscreen stated Ye Olde Tin Can. The bus was fitted out with about fourteen red wickerwork seats, with red leather cushions.

A board on the slaughterhouse of T.D. Dennis in High Street and a notice in chalk informed Ashwell that 'Ye Olde Tin Can' would leave at 5.30 p.m. on Sundays bound for Bedford, Henlow and Hitchin, returning about 10.30 p.m.

This was soon followed by a service to London every Friday. The next step was the purchase of two Dennis coaches, which were used for seaside outings, exhibitions, shows, etc. Henry drove one coach and Bob Cole, his brother-in-law, the other. Spurred on by the success of the coach business, Henry then considered a daily bus service from Hitchin to Cambridge via Letchworth, Baldock, Ashwell, the Mordens, Royston and all the villages to Cambridge, with early morning buses for workers and a late night bus from Hitchin on Saturdays for cinemagoers. All of this came to pass.

There were very few cars in those days, so it really put sleepy old Ashwell on the map. With more buses, it was necessary to build garages and a workshop. F.J. Bailey & Co did the building work and were able to make use of a range of large window frames which had been removed during the alterations at Ashwell Bury. With extra buses, extra drivers and a mechanic were needed. To house them, two cottages were built at West End by Baileys and another pair in Back Street by W.F. Rand, another Ashwell builder.

It was not very long before one of the big bus companies cast their greedy eyes on our bus service. They threatened to run Henry off the road; he was compelled to sell out, and Ashwell lost its Cockney hat manufacturer-cum-bus proprietor.

Aston Ayres (who was, I believe, a nephew of the novelist, Ruby M. Ayres) and was late of the Royal Flying Corps, came to Ashwell soon after the war. He married one of the daughters of George Chalkley and rented some of the wooden sheds alongside the river at the mill in Mill Street. He was a clever engineer, did some engine and motor repairs, and was at the fore-front when wireless - the one and two valve variety with wet and dry batteries - came into being. Yet Aston Ayres is best remembered for his cinemas.

Until he came to Ashwell it was a lengthy and expensive business to see a film. We could cycle to Ashwell station (no buses in those days) and catch a train to see the film at either the small cinema at Baldock, the Palace cinema at Letchworth or the Playhouse at Hitchin, where I remember seeing "Ben Hur", silent of course. Nevertheless, special films like this had sound effects. From behind the scenes came the rattle of chains as the slaves were whipped, the shaking of a sheet of metal for the noise of the chariots. And how we laughed when the sounds did not coincide with the film. If we did not wish to go by train the alternative was to cycle to either of the three towns.

Aston Ayres opened his first cinema at Ashwell Village Hall about 1923 or 24; at first just two performances on Saturday evenings with Kenneth Bryant at the piano, watching the film and at the same time trying to play suitable music to fit the picture. The cinema was very successful. With people coming in from the other villages, it was soon necessary to have matinees for the children. From this small beginning Ayres went on to take over the old Baldock cinema, followed by building the Astonia cinema opposite Kayser Bondor factor, now Tesco's superstore, and then on to Stevenage, where he built another. Sadly, all three have gone.

Until Henry Leverett began his bus service Ashwell's only public transport was by horse-drawn vehicle. George Strickland, a retired baker who lived in Silver Street, used a pony and trap for short journeys such as the two and a half miles to Ashwell station. If pressed, he would make the seven mile journey to Royston market. But the main means of travel was by horse and fly, a smart, enclosed vehicle owned and driven by Mynot Reynolds or his daughter-in-law, Mrs Charles Reynolds, who lived near the Springs. Mrs John Bonfield of the Bushel and Strike inn also had a horse-drawn vehicle. The first car used for taxi work was owned by Fred Dellar, a brother of Charles, the crippled greengrocer. Fred at that time lived in the now derelict thatched cottage near Blugegates dairy. The car was, as far as I recall, a second-hand American Chevrolet.

I remember quite clearly one Sunday in 1917 or 1918 when my grandparents hired Fred with his motor-car to take a party of Sheldricks to visit their relatives first at Thriplow, Cambridgeshire and in the afternoon to see Great-aunt Mariane, my grandfather's sister, at Heydon, Essex. In the churchyard she pointed out a man wearing a panama hat and grey suit. She said it was Lord Braybrooke of Audley End. At the time I didn't believe her, because he looked just the same as other men! We left Ashwell early that morning. I think we saw two lorries with soldiers, and three other cars during the whole of the day, and arrived back well past my bedtime.

Fred Dellar later built a bungalow on the Hinxworth road. At that time American-made cars were shipped over here in heavy wooden containers. Fred bought some of these from which he built his bungalow - known as El Rancho, now owned by Gordon and Marjorie Gentle, who also are engaged in transport as Gentles Coaches. The bungalow has been considerably enlarged and is fully brick clad.

Alf Ketteridge, with his garage and taxi in High Street, I mentioned much earlier. The garage has since been replaced by two houses next to Stella House.

One other form of transport was the Great Northern Railway's horse-drawn van, driven by Sam Mayes. Sam delivered huge sacks (known in the brewing trade as hop pockets) of Kentish hops to the brewery. His van also carried wooden boxes of Tate & Lyle's sugar, huge wrapped cheeses (two to a crate), blocks of salt: in fact, most of the goods sold in Ashwell's shops.

All sorts of people were buying and selling all sorts of things. A young Baldock man with a peaked cap pushed a cycle with a heavy insulated box in front selling Walls icecream, "snow fruits" - a sort of coloured lump of ice - for one penny or a vanilla ice cream wafer for twopence. The Walls slogan was "Stop me and buy one". Very soon there was a rival in the Eldorado icecream man.

There were buyers of old iron, rags and rabbit-skins, collectors of jam jars; a 2lb jam jar or two 1lb jars were worth a windmill for the children. I remember a dark-skinned man playing a hurdy-gurdy with a monkey sitting on his shoulder, gipsy women selling pegs and telling fortunes and gipsy men grinding knives and scissors.

The Lord Kitchener

On the Saturday before the first Sunday in July, an enterprising young man came over from Stotfold with his horse and trap selling new potatoes and green peas. He knew that it was an old Ashwell custom to eat new potatoes and peas on the first Sunday in July to celebrate the coming of Ashwell Feast.

The children were more interested in the fair than the food. After morning Sunday school it was important to be at the recreation ground in time to see the first caravans arrive from Melbourn where the fair had ended the previous night. Then came the big steam engine, Lord Kitchener, towing a huge wagon loaded with all the bits and pieces which made up James Harris and Sons flying horses, soon followed by Viscount Lascelles, a slightly smaller engine, towing more of the fair equipment. By midday most of the fair had arrived, the water tap near the Cricketers pub had been connected to supply water for the horses, the engines and the caravan people. Soon the caravan chimneys were smoking as the fair people's meal was being prepared, and the Ashwell children drifted homewards to their meat and two veg, new potatoes and green peas and to prepare for the two days' school holiday which had always been granted for Ashwell Feast.

It was only a small fair. The Harris's came from Biggleswade and Jim's wife was one of the Wren family, the Biggleswade fishmongers. Jim's brother drove the Lord Kitchener which provided power for most of the fair's lighting, powered the flying horses, and the organ with its figures automatically banging drums and playing flutes and other instruments, blasting out such popular tunes as "Valencia" and "I'm one of the nuts from Barcelona". Every now and then, just to hurry patrons along, there was an almighty shriek on the whistle, which could be heard all over the village.

The Harris girls, blonde and smartly dressed, attracted the customers to the dart stalls and a shooting gallery where you fired corks at packets of Woodbine cigarettes, boxes of Swan Vesta matches and other twopenny items. Young Jim Harris was usually the caller at a set of large faces with open mouths and clay pipes instead of teeth. You threw three wooden balls for twopence in an attempt to smash the "teeth". A sign above the children's roundabouts announced that Mannings Amusements were the owners, and a little man with a little moustache would collect the kids' pennies, then wearily turn a handle which sent the whole machine revolving. At Mr Smith's shooting gallery a sign informed the marksman that it was three shots for twopence, and in the unlikely event of a win there were packets of cheap cigarettes and toys. You took aim at a ping-pong ball which was gently rising and falling on a tiny fountain of water. It appeared to be a mile away, but actually was about thirty feet.

Mr Smith's son was in charge of a dart saloon. Sally Shaw and her two sons came from Thriplow in Cambridgeshire. Sally had a rock and confectionery stall, which was craftily situated at the fair entrance to catch the eyes of the children, both as they arrived and as they were about to leave. There were long square sticks of peppermint, pineapple and raspberry flavoured rocks, neatly stacked; brandysnaps and pink and white almond nougat.

As the electric lights were switched on over the Harris Amusements and side shows, the Smiths and Shaws lit their evil smelling naphtha oil flares. The two young Shaws looked like a couple of Chicago gangsters, with their black felt trilbys and flash suits. One ran the coconut shy, the other the skittles. The heavy wooden skittles, weighted with lead, were whitewashed and were set up in pyramids for the player to knock over with light wooden balls.

From time to time there was a sideshow. I remember seeing a lady without a body; just head, shoulders and arms were visible. There was an African chief who was a fire eater and danced barefoot on broken glass while shouting in a strange tongue. But when he spoke to the lady who collected the entrance fees he had a Liverpool accent and they had a half caste young son.

To our cricketers Ashwell Feast Monday and Tuesday brought the highlight of the season, a two-day match, Ashwell versus Dr (later Sir Comyns) Berkeley's team of young doctors from the Middlesex Hospital. In the cemetery, a stone's-throw away from the cricket field, there is a stone slab, overgrown and covered with lichen, to the memory of Comyns Berkeley, Knight Bachelor, died 1946, and to his wife Dame Ethel, last surviving daughter of Edward King Fordham of Ashwell Bury, who died in 1945. For a good many years a distinguished pupil of Sir Comyns lived at Townsend Close on the other side of the cricket field - Mr. O.V. Lloyd-Davies, F.R.C.S., surgeon, who died in 1987 aged 82. The "Times" obituary states that he devised many instruments for his speciality, and that he was responsible for certain treatments which greatly eased the lot of the cancer patient. One of today's team of doctors - Rino Coladangelo - was also trained at the Middlesex Hospital.

Schools and School Teachers

The Ashwell Board schools were built in 1878. Charles Walkden was one of those appointed to the board and was highly amused when a man from a neighbouring village explained that they did not need a Board school because they had a perfectly good brick one!

The door on the left was the entrance to the girls' school, the door on the right led into the mixed infants' school which I entered in 1915 at the age of four. I can see Miss Stewart, the teacher, now, with her golden hair and pink blouse. The new boys and girls were entered in the register and then seated on one of the gallery steps where, among other things, we were taught such simple things as stitching a button to a piece of cloth, knitting a tiny woollen square, and writing letters and figures on a slate. We watched the buds bursting on chestnut twigs placed in water in tall glass vases, and in the autumn and winter hyacinth bulbs shooting and flowering in the same glass vases.

In the twenties the Board schools were in exactly the same condition as when they were built in 1878 - plain distempered walls above dark stained and varnished matchboarding. Doors and roof timbers were also stained and varnished, boarded floors scrubbed occasionally. High window cills prevented distraction and a draughty range of outside toilets froze solid in hard winters. The playground was gravelled and uneven. Indeed the schools remained in about the same condition until 1946. (In the twenties Miss Anne Hyslop became the headmistress and Miss Annie Bray was in charge of the infants.)

When we reached our seventh birthday we said farewell to Miss Stewart. The girls then climbed the steps to the door on the left where they were to receive the rest of their education up to the age of fourteen, under Miss Chambers, the headmistress, and her teachers, unless their parents could afford to send them to Hitchin Grammar School.

In those days getting there was quite an ordeal. It entailed cycling the two and a half miles to Ashwell station, whatever the weather, to catch a train around 8 a.m. followed by a long walk to the school and of course the reverse journey after 4 p.m. On the other hand, the children at Ashwell schools went home for the midday meal. Attendance at grammar school meant sandwiches - no school meals in those days. The boys' future was a little more uncertain. There had been rumours of caning at the Merchant Taylors' school, so it was with some apprehension that our little party of boys from the infant school reported to Mr Chote, the headmaster, who quickly passed us on to his daughter.

Miss Madelene Chote was responsible for the new intake. For some years she had watched her new boys grow into men and join the forces, and each week she scanned the list of those killed in action published in the "Royston Crow", then hurried round to comfort mothers and wives. Miss Chote cared so much for her boys: she wrote a patriotic poem, which was published in a national magazine, after a copy had been accepted by Queen Alexandra.

This may account for the fact that on the walls of the main classroom hung coloured portraits of King Edward VII (although King George V had been on the throne for seven years) and Queen Alexandra.

The old classrooms had been tidied up and the large new room built in 1876, with high window cills, boarded floors and undecorated red bricks walls. The open fire provided heat for Mr Chote, whose reign as headmaster lasted from 1876 to 1918, and those pupils in one half of the room, whilst those in the other half shivered. Miss Chote stayed on after her father retired to Hitchin in 1918.

Mr Morgan Biles was the new headmaster and Gwendoline, his elder daughter, a teacher, whilst Aileen, the younger daughter, helped out at times.

Apart from the royal portraits a large board adorned the wall behind the Head's chair. It bore the names of the annual winners of the Gentle silver cup. Sir William Gentle, an old boy of the school had presented the cup; there was also an old map of the British Isles, but several large frames, containing the photographs of young soldiers, sailors and airmen, had been Mr Chote's pride and joy.

When the war ended, Mr Biles had hoped to put up something colourful. He took down the photographs, placed them in envelopes and returned them to wives or parents. So loyal were the people of Ashwell to Mr Chote and so upset at the removal of the photographs, that John Worboys, the town crier, was sent out to proclaim a public meeting, to be addressed by Mr Chote. The meeting demanded that the old boys' photographs were returned to the school walls. So they remained until after World War Two, when they were placed in a large album and deposited at Ashwell museum.

Apart from the heavy pitchpine and cast-iron framed six-seater desks, the school furniture consisted of teachers' desks, a few chairs, an ancient American harmonium, two old revolving globes, which were out of date by 1919, blackboards and easels, a cupboard in each room and a clock made by John Bennett of London on the wall behind the Head's desk.

In the cupboards were three sets of well-worn reading books - "The Swiss Family Robinson", "Nat the Naturalist" and "The Black Arrow", and a few Bibles. Our reading and spelling lessons were mainly from these books. The Bible, the wise Mr. Biles told us, contained every word that we would ever need. Each day Mr Biles brought in the "Daily Mail", and on Thursdays Arthur Mee's "Children's Newspaper", both of which we used for reading and spelling.

One half-day each week we spent at the Technical Room with Mr Firth, the woodwork master, who cycled over from Royston, and Friday afternoons were spent on the school gardens in Gardiners Lane with Mr Biles. He was not only a good teacher, but good at gardening and his great hobby was cricket. Ashwell Choral & Dramatic Society met under his supervision and provided quite a bit of entertainment in the village hall.

There appeared to be just one scholarship place each year at Hitchin Boys' Grammar School.

Mr William Appleton lived in some style with his wife, son and daughter at The Red House, now Townsend Close. Mrs Appleton drove her husband to and from the station daily. He was always immaculately dressed - either a grey Anthony Eden hat or a bowler, smart suit and blue overcoat with a touch of velvet on the collar. On Armistice Sundays he wore a medal of some kind, suspended round his neck by a purple ribbon. After Mr Appleton became a trustee of our museum, he presented a copy of a book which he had written "What We Want and Where We Are". From this book we learned that he was Secretary to the General Federation of Trades Unions.

Another of our trustees was Henry Bowman, who knew a great deal of Ashwell and its past, but unfortunately did not record it. He lived at the Lychens (now Little Garth) in Mill Street until 1920 when he moved to Letchworth. There he became chairman of the magistrates, but still retained a great interest in Ashwell.

At Little Garth, you can still see the section of wall cut away to give Henry Bowman an unhindered view of the junction of Swan Street with Mill Street where he imagined the market cross stood. At one time he undertook excavations in a meadow near Loves farm, which was in the area of Glytton, Ashwell's lost hamlet. Stained glass was found from which he deduced that there had been a chapel dedicated to St Peter.

One Penny.

THE

Ashwell Snowdrop Minstrels.

PROGRAMME

OF AN

ENTERTAINMENT

TO BE GIVEN IN THE

COUNTY COUNCIL SCHOOLROOM,

ASHWELL,

ON

FRIDAY, April 11, 1913,

COMMENCING AT 8 O'CLOCK SHARP.

BONES.	TAMBOS.
HERB. PACK,	J. DAVIS,
H. P. PACK,	W. RAND,
C. PACK.	G. HOLLOWAY.

MUSICAL DIRECTOR: MR. G. F. PACK.

PART I.

OPENING CHORUS	... ...	The Troupe.
SONG	... "It's just like bein' at Hame" ...	P. Anderson.
COMIC SONG	"I saw Peter Henry Home" ...	G. Holloway.
SONG	... ...	G. Smith.
COMIC SONG	"Kiss the Girl if you are going to"	J. Davis.
SONG	... ... "Mamie May" ...	V. Chapman.
COMIC SONG	"Another little Girl for Charlie"	H. Pack.
SONG	... ... "Go to Sea" ...	G. Lawman.
COMIC SONG	"Come and cut a piece of Cake"	W. Rand.
SONG	... ... "Old Sun-bonnet" ...	M. Kirchin.
COMIC SONG	... "Elegant Bertie" ...	C. Pack.
SONG	"When they ask you what your name is"	A. Canfield.
COMIC SONG	... "Serves you Right" ...	H. P. Pack.
SONG	... "I am alone" ...	E. Martin.
FINALE & MARCH	... ...	The Troupe.

Interval of 5 Minutes.

PART II.

COMIC SONG	... ...	W. Rand.
SONG	... ...	W. Whylie.
COMIC SONG	"Rings on my Fingers"	C. Eversden.

SKETCH IN ONE ACT

Entitled:—

'Waxination Gratis.'

CHARACTERS:—

SIGNOR FRANGIPANI	A. CANFIELD
LONG JIM	G. DAVIS.
DEAF JOE	HERB. PACK.
MR. HANNIBAL WASHINGTON ...	GEO. SMITH.
GREENACRE GREENEYE ...	G. HOLLOWAY.
DETECTIVE BULLSEYE	G. LAWMAN.
MRS. GREENEYE	P. SHELDRICK.
AND	
BOB	H. P. PACK.

GOD SAVE THE KING.

The Ashwell Snowdrops – a concert party of Ashwell men – performed regularly pre 1914. One of their programmes is reproduced here in reduced size.. (Museum)

ASHWELL CORONATION MEMORIAL.

The Committee propose to make a Permanent Memorial of the Coronation at the Springs, and with the adjoining garden owned by Messrs. E. K. & H. Fordham, who offer to lease it to the Parish, at a nominal rent of a few shillings per year. The Committee appeal for subscriptions to lay out some walks, provide seats, plant the banks of the Springs with inexpensive shrubs and foliage and carry out other improvements for a place of enjoyment, to better appreciate the beauty of the Spings.

12—**Three Legged Race Handicap—100 yds.** 1st, Prize, two Writing Cases; 2nd, two Post Card Albums; 3rd, two Coronation Purses, 4th, two Boxes Dominoes.

5-40 FIRST HEAT.	5-50 SECOND HEAT.
A. Mole and L. Pack, scratch	J. Reavell and W. Randall, scratch.
F. Potton and P. Wilkins, 5yds	E. Hyder and H. Gceves, 5 yds.
H. Picking and A. Wilkins 5 yds.	J. Chapman and L. Wilsher, 10 yds.
C. Smith and A. Brown, 10 yds.	H. Willmott and A. Beale, 15 yds.
S. Sheldrick and F. Sheldrick, 10 yds.	E. Brown and H. Gallant, 15 yds.
C. Searle and S. Edwards 15 yds.	H. Bryant and T. Goss, 15 yds.

13—**Final Boys under 10.**
6-0.

14—**Final Gentle Challenge Cup.**
6-10.

15—**Old Boys Race Handicap—Quarter Mile.** 1st Prize, Mug Presented by Mr. H. W. Bowman, 2nd, Sugar Scuttle, 3rd, Shaving Mirror etc; 4th, Razor
6-15.

16—**Final Three Legged Race.**
6-30.

17—**Final Potato Race.**
6-35.

18—**Final Wheel-barrow Race.**
6-45.

19—**CLIMBING GREASY POLE.** 1st, Prize, Leg of Mutton; 2nd, Carvers; 3rd, Watch.

OTHER EVENTS, &c., &c.,
as the Committee may be able to arrange.

PRESENTATION OF PRIZES.

The Committee may have to make some slight alterations and other events may be added.

GOD SAVE THE KING.

ASHWELL
Coronation Celebration.

JUNE 22nd, 1911.

EXECUTIVE COMMITTEE:
*W. A. Fordham, Esq. (Chairman), *Mrs. W. A. Fordham, Miss Chote, Mrs. Pag e, Messrs. *J, W. Bailey, *H. W. Bowman (Vice-chairman) B. Bryant, A. W. Chote, *W. Cooper, J. Page, J. W. Pack (Hon. Treas.), J. Rogers, *T. Wylie and *J. P. Goble (Hon. Sec.)
**These members are Committee for the Permanent Memorial.*

SUBSCRIPTION COMMITTEE:
Mrs. Page, Mrs. J. W. Bailey, Miss Chote, Messrs. B. Bryant, H. W. Bowman, A. W. Chote and J. W. Bailey (Hon. Sec.)

TEA COMMITTEE:
Mrs. W. A. Fordham, Mrs. J. W. Bailey, Miss Chote, Miss Cooper, Miss S. J. Pack, Mrs. Page, Miss M. Sale, Mrs. Weigall and Miss Wylie.

The Committee announce the following arrangements:

Divine Service at 11 a.m. in the Parish Church.

SPORTS 2·30 p.m.

1. Merchant Taylors' School Sports. 2. Village Sports.

To be held in a meadow at Westbury, by kind permission of Messrs. B. & A. Christy

BASSINGBOURN CHURCH BRASS BAND
will play Selections of Music.

A TEA will be provided for Children under 15 and for Adults over 60 years of age. Admission by Ticket only.

Mrs. W. A. Fordham has kindly promised an Entertainment of the

MORRIS DANCES.

DANCING ON THE GREEN.

The Committee after much consideration decided to abandon the proposed Bonfire.

Tea 6d. each by Mr. L. Day. Fruit and Sweet Stall, D. Dellar.

GOD SAVE THE KING.

Part of the 1911 Coronation Celebration Programme.. (Museum)

Ashwell people dress up in all their finery to celebrate the 1911 Coronation at a party given by Mr Joshua Page of Page's Brewery. The Barn is at the rear of 110 High Street. Just see those hats! (Museum)

THE VILLAGE HALL,
ASHWELL.

COMIC OPERA

"ERMINIE"

(HARRY aad EDWARD PAULTON and JACOBOWSKI).

By

The Ashwell Choral and Dramatic Society.

Wednesday & Thursday JANUARY 21st & 22nd, 1931.	Welcome! Welcome to the Fête! 'Tis of graciousness an act we Thoroughly appreciate. At village feast, here meeting you, With duteous service greeting you, With cheery voice repeating, you Are welcome to our fête.	Monday & Tuesday, JANUARY 26th & 27th, 1931.

Nightly at 7.30 p.m. ∵ Doors Open 7 p.m.

SEATS (Including Tax):

Numbered and Reserved - - - 2/6 and 1/6.

Unreserved 9d.

School Children half-price.

Seats may be booked daily at Ashwell Post Office.

Previous Productions: "Xmas in the Olden Time" (Twice), "Aladdin," "Don Quixote," "Ali Baba," "Cupid and the Ogre," "Phillida" and "Cecelia."

NOTICE Ladies are respectfully requested to remove their hats at the rise of the Curtain.

PROGRAMME TWOPENCE.

Ashwell Choral and Dramatic Society, founded by Mr M. Biles, Headmaster of Merchant Taylors School, about 1923.
Composed entirely of young Ashwell men and women, they put on excellent performances at the Village Hall.
(Museum)

Ashwell v. Royston Nonconformist Young Men's Society.—A match between the above was played at Ashwell yesterday (Thursday), when the visitors were defeated by 42 runs on the 1st innings. Score:—

ASHWELL.

	1st inns.		2nd inns.
G. Winter, b Pool	11	b Pool	10
S. Hyde, c Wilson	3	run out	7
H. Wright, b Pool	10	b Pool	0
P. Pack, c Bush, b Pepper	9	not out	15
S. Winter, b Bush	31	run out	6
Walter Rand, b Pepper	4	c Pepper, b Pool	0
J. Oyston, c and b Wilson	17	run out	2
V. Angell, b Pepper	4		
F. Bailey, b Bush	6		
B. Bailey, b Pepper	3		
G. R. Fordham, not out	0		
Extras	11	Extras	11
	109		51

ROYSTON N.Y.M.S.

A. Pepper, c Oyston, b G. Winter	2
P. Fisher, b Hyde	25
A. Wilson, c Hyde, b Pack	3
H. Pool, b Hyde	23
G. Beale, b Hyde	1
F. Wilson, b Hyde	0
L. Mortimer, b Hyde	1
R. Humphrey, c Rand	11
C. Carrington, b S. Winter	1
A. Bush, c Rand, b Hyde	0

Top: *Sir Comyns Berkeley's cricket team of young doctors from the Middlesex Hospital played Ashwell during the Feast week. (c.1900)* (Author)
Back Row: *The Hospital Team umpire Len Haylock*
Centre Row: *3. Mr Gale (Schoolmaster), 4. Gus Moss, 6. Wolverley Fordham, 7. Sir Comyns Berkeley, 9. John Bailey (Builder).*
Seated: *1. Sam Winter (Landlord of the Horse & Groom pub on A505)*

Left: *Royston Crow, May 1901.* (Museum)

Below: *Ashwell 1920s Cricket Team* (Museum)
Back Row l to r: *Umpire John Worboys, Shopkeeper & Town Crier; Scorer Sonny Westerman; Fred Westrope of Westrope's shop; Russell Fordham; Albert Furr; -----?; Hubert Radford, Carpenter & Joiner; John Anderson, Building worker.*
Seated l to r: *J.R. Burton, Chemist; -----?; Charles Westrope, Grocer; Lawrence Pack, Farmer; Morgan Biles, Headmaster Merchant Taylors School; Stanley Bryant, Coalmerchant's Clerk.*

Above: *Ashwell Hockey team, 1914*
Back Row l to r: *Mr Goble, Jack Bonfield, L. Pack, Jack Worboys, Mr Gale, ----? Martin.*
Front Row l to r: *Sam Bonfield, Stan Pack, ----? Bullard, ----? Day.*
(Museum/Stan Bryant)

ASHWELL

FLOWER SHOW

AND

• FÊTE •

To be held on

August Bank Holiday

(Monday 2nd August, 1937).

AT

Elbrook, Ashwell.

President: Colonel EUSTACE HILL, D.S.O.

COMMITTEE:

Dr. J. H. Moynihan (Chairman), Mrs. R. Covington, Mrs. W. A. Fordham, J.P., Messrs. F. Pettengell, W. Searle, G. C. Whitby, S. Whitehead, W. G. Whitehead, W. J. Whitehead, W. E. Barrow and C. C. Levitt (Joint Hon. Secretaries).

SUBSCRIPTIONS:

Hon. Treasurer—Mr. C. C. Levitt, Windyside, Station Road, Ashwell, Herts.

Elphick, Printer, Biggleswade.

Left: *Front cover of the August Bank Holiday Show in 1937, when it fell on the 1st Monday in August. Note the Printers – Elphick, still going in 1991.*

Opposite Page: *The Rules and Regulations and List of Classes and Prizes, which make very interesting reading.*
(Museum)

RULES AND REGULATIONS.

1.—A Subscriber of 2/6 shall be entitled to a ticket of free admission to the Grounds and a Subscriber of 5/- and over to two tickets, on presentation of his receipt at the gate.

2.—The Show shall consist of four Divisions as defined in the Schedule.

3.—There shall be an entrance of 3d. for exhibiting in each class in each separate Division, but anyone exhibiting in more than four classes in such Division shall be entitled to free entrance in any other classes in the Division. SCHOOL ENTRIES when sent to Secretary *en bloc* entrance 1d. for each separate exhibit in each class. *All Entrance Fees must be paid previous to Entry.*

4.—Every Exhibitor shall declare that his or her exhibits are of their own growing, preparation or manufacture. Any person evading this rule shall forfeit all prizes and be disqualified from showing in future. The Committee shall have the right to inspect produce entered for exhibition.

5.—All exhibits must be brought to the Show Ground between the hours of 8 o'clock and 11 o'clock on the morning of the Show.

6.—Exhibitors must provide their own plates and dishes and other receptacles for exhibits, and nothing must be removed from the Show till 7 p.m.

7.—No Exhibitor shall take more than 30 shillings in Prize money.

8.—Three prizes will only be given where there are Six Exhibitors in a class. Where there are less than Six, prizes will be given on merit only, and may be withheld at the discretion of the Judges.

9.—All protests or disputes shall be referred to the Committee in writing before 7 p.m. on the day of Exhibition, and their decision shall be final.

10.—Entry Forms will be received at the Technical Room, Swan Street, Ashwell, Herts., between 7 p.m. and 9 p.m. on Thursday, 29th and Friday, 30th July, 1937, or by post, *including remittance* to cover entrance fees (Cheques and Postal Orders crossed "Barclays Bank, Ltd.") to: Mr. C. C. Levitt, Hon. Secretary, Windyside, Station Road, Ashwell, Herts.

11.—**ON NO ACCOUNT WILL ENTRIES BE RECEIVED ON THE GROUND.**

LIST OF CLASSES AND PRIZES.

DIVISION A.

Open to Cottagers only, within a radius of 5 miles, who have not in any previous show won prizes to the value of 20/-.

Class		Prizes 1st	2nd	3rd
1	Collection of Vegetables (4 distinct kinds)	7/6	4/6	3/6
2	Six Potatoes (Kidney) on plate	4/-	3/-	1/6
3	Six Potatoes (Round) on plate	4/-	3/-	1/6
4	Twelve Pods of Peas	2/6	1/6	1/-
5	Twelve Pods of Broad Beans (Long)	2/6	1/6	1/-
5a	Twelve Pods of Broad Beans (Short)	2/6	1/6	1/-
6	Twelve Runner Beans	2/6	1/6	1/-
7	Two Marrows	2/6	1/6	1/-
8	Six Carrots	2/6	1/6	1/-
9	Six Onions (Spring) taken from bed	2/6	1/6	1/-
10	Six Onions (Winter)	2/6	1/6	1/-
11	Six Turnips	2/6	1/6	1/-
12	Three Lettuces (Cos)	2/6	1/6	1/-
13	Three Lettuces (Cabbage)	2/6	1/6	1/-
14	Three Cabbages	2/6	1/6	1/-
15	Collection of Fruit (4 varieties)	4/-	3/-	2/-
16	Four Vases of Cut (outdoor) Flowers (distinct) (Annuals, Perennials, or both)	4/-	3/-	2/-
17	One Vase of Flowers (mixed)	3/-	2/-	1/-
18	One Vase of Sweet Peas (mixed)	3/-	2/-	1/-
19	Three Roses (distinct)	3/-	2/-	1/-
20	Dahlias, Giant, four cut blooms in vase ..	3/-	2/-	1/-
21	Dahlias, any other variety, six cut blooms in vase	3/-	2/-	1/-

DIVISION B.

Open to Cottagers and Amateurs (not being Gardeners or employing a Gardener solely in that capacity) within a radius of 5 miles.

Class		Prizes 1st	2nd	3rd
22	Collection of Vegetables (6 distinct kinds) ..	7/6	4/6	3/6
23	Fifteen Pods of Peas	2/6	1/6	1/-
24	Fifteen Pods of Broad Beans	2/6	1/6	1/-
25	Fifteen Runner Beans	2/6	1/6	1/-
26	Two Marrows	2/6	1/6	1/-
27	Six Carrots	2/6	1/6	1/-
28	Six Onions (Spring)	2/6	1/6	1/-
29	Six Onions (Winter)	2/6	1/6	1/-
30	Six Turnips	2/6	1/6	1/-
31	Six Potatoes (Kidney) on plate	3/-	2/-	1/-
32	Six Potatoes (Round) on plate	3/-	2/-	1/-
33	Twelve Outdoor-grown Tomatoes	3/-	2/-	1/-
34	Collection of Fruit (4 varieties)	4/-	3/-	2/-
35	Four Roses (distinct)	4/-	2/6	1/6
36	Sweet Peas (4 vases distinct, 6 stems in each)	4/-	2/6	1/6
37	Four Vases of Cut (outdoor) Flowers (distinct) (Annuals, Perennials, or both)	4/-	2/6	1/6
38	Six Carnations (not less than 3 varieties) ..	3/-	2/-	1/-
39	Best arranged Two Vases of Flowers (mixed)	3/-	2/-	1/-
40	Dahlias, Giant, four cut blooms in vase ..	3/-	2/-	1/-
41	Dahlias, any other variety, six cut blooms in vase	3/-	2/-	1/-

DIVISION C.

Open to all within a radius of 9 miles.

Class		Prizes 1st	2nd	3rd
42	Collection of Vegetables (8 distinct kinds) ..	10/6	7/6	5/-
43	Fifteen Pods of Peas	2/6	1/6	1/-
44	Fifteen Pods of Broad Beans	2/6	1/6	1/-
45	Fifteen Runner Beans	2/6	1/6	1/-
46	Nine Potatoes (Kidney)	3/-	2/-	1/-
47	Nine Potatoes (Round)	3/-	2/-	1/-
48	Six Onions (Spring)	3/-	2/-	1/-
49	Six Onions (Winter)	3/-	2/-	1/-
50	Six Carrots	3/-	2/-	1/-
51	Twelve Tomatoes (underglass)	3/-	2/-	1/-
52	Three Cucumbers (underglass)	3/-	2/-	1/-
53	Collection of outdoor Fruit (4 varieties) ..	7/6	4/6	3/-
54	Six Roses (distinct)	5/-	3/6	2/-
55	Six Carnations (not less than 3 varieties) ..	4/-	3/-	2/-
56	Sweet Peas (4 vases distinct, 6 stems in each)	4/-	2/6	1/6
57	Three Vases of Gladioli (distinct)	3/-	2/-	1/-
58	Four Vases Perennial Flowers (distinct) ..	4/-	3/-	2/-
59	Four Vases Annual Flowers (distinct)	4/-	3/-	2/-
60	Dahlias, Giant, four cut blooms in vase ..	4/-	3/-	2/-
61	Dahlias, any other variety, six cut blooms in vase	4/-	3/-	2/-

DIVISION D.

Open to all within a radius of 5 miles.

Class		Prizes 1st	2nd	3rd
62	Best Hand Knitted Pair Socks	3/-	2/-	1/-
63	Best Hand Knitted Garment	3/-	2/-	1/-
64	Best Wool Mat or Rug (Handmade)	4/-	3/-	2/-
65	Best Article in Fancy Needlework	4/-	3/-	2/-
66	Any Article Handwork	4/-	3/-	2/-
67	White Bread (2lb. Cottage Loaf, made from British Flour)	4/-	3/-	2/-
68	Brown Bread (2lb. Cottage Loaf, made from British Flour)	4/-	3/-	2/-
69	Jam, 1lb. Pot (1937 Preserve)	2/6	1/6	1/-
70	Jelly, 1lb. Pot (1937 Preserve)	2/6	1/6	1/-
71	Orange Marmalade, 1lb. Pot (1937 Preserve)	2/6	1/6	1/-
72	One Bottle Pickles (1936-1937 Preserve) ..	2/6	1/6	1/-
73	Bottled Fruit (2 Bottles distinct, 1937 Preserve)	3/-	2/-	1/-
74	Best Nine Boiled Potatoes	3/-	2/-	1/-
75	Best Working Man's Dinner, not to cost over 9d. (in dish)	3/-	2/-	1/-
76	Best Exhibit Home-made Sweets	2/6	1/6	1/-
77	Sponge Sandwich	3/-	2/-	1/-
78	Cake (from this receipe only)	4/-	3/-	2/-

FRUIT CAKE.

½lb. Butter, ½lb. Sugar, 1lb. Mixed Fruit, 3 or 4 Eggs, 6ozs. Self-Raising Flour, 6ozs. Plain Flour.

Additional prizes will be awarded by Messrs. C. Day & Son, Ashwell, to those prizewinners using their brand of Self-Raising Flour.

Class		Prizes 1st	2nd	3rd
79	Three Sections Honey	3/-	2/-	1/-
80	Two 1lb. Pots (screw tops) Run Honey ..	3/-	2/-	1/-

OPEN TO CHILDREN under 15 years.

Class		Prizes 1st	2nd	3rd
81	Best arranged Collection Wild Flowers (under 11 years)	2/6	1/6	1/-
82	Best arranged Collection Wild Flowers (under 15 years)	2/6	1/6	1/-
83	Best Article, Plain Needlework (under 11 years)	3/-	2/-	1/-
84	Best Article, Plain Needlework (under 15 years)	3/-	2/-	1/-
85	Best Article, Fancy Needlework (under 11 years)	3/-	2/-	1/-
86	Best Article, Fancy Needlework (under 15 years)	3/-	2/-	1/-
87	Best Exhibit Leatherwork	3/-	2/-	1/-
88	Best Specimens of Handicraft (boys under 13 years)	3/-	2/-	1/-
89	Best Specimen of Handicraft (boys under 15 years)	3/-	2/-	1/-
90	Best Exhibit Handwork other than specified	3/-	2/-	1/-

Ashwell Choral and Dramatic Society, Village Hall, early 1930s. (The Comet Newspaper/Mr & Mrs P. Howes)
Standing l to r: *N. Howes, -----?, Mrs B. Wallace, K. Bryant, Mrs Seymour, Mrs N. Howes, -----?, Mrs C. Harradine.*
Seated: *W. James, W. Huffer, Miss M. Barrow, -----?*

Centre Left *Young Ashwellians on Cromer beach in 1929. A different world from topless bathing!!* (Mrs B. Wallace)

Above: *Ashwell ladies after enjoying a paddle at Yarmouth in 1920. L-R: Mrs S. Waldock, Mrs A. Goss, Mrs W. Wilkins, Mrs S. Bullard, Mrs E.Webb, Mrs A. Parrish, Miss L.Westerman, -----? (Mr & Mrs H. Bullard)*

Left: *Cars lined up round the ring at the Annual Bank Holiday Show in 1929. This shot has been enlarged by over 300%.*(Mrs B. Wallace)

For Home and Country.

ASHWELL WOMEN'S INSTITUTE.

Programme for 1928.

President—	Vice-President—	Hon. Treasurer—	Hon. Secretary—
Mrs. R. Seymour.	Mrs. W. A. Fordham.	Mrs. J. R. Burton, The Pharmacy, Ashwell.	Mrs. A. N. Howes, Westbury Cottage, Ashwell.

Committee—

Mrs. Barrow, (C).	Miss G. Burton, (E).	Mrs. Goss, (E).	Mrs. Wilkins, (E).
Mrs. Barton, (R).	Mrs. H. Christy (R).	Mrs. C. Harradine, (E).	Miss Wylie, (E).
Miss Biles, (E).	Miss M. Christy (R).	Miss Huggins (C).	
Mrs. W. A. Bray (R).	Mrs. Clements (R).	Miss Hyslop, (R).	

Sub-Committees—R = Refreshment. E = Entertainment. C = Competition.

Jan. 19th—*"If you would reach the mark—aim high!"*
A Travel Talk—Miss A. W. Hyslop.
Competition—Best peeled potato in one minute blindfold.
Roll Call—My favourite Song.
Entertainment - Community Singing.

Feb. 16th.—*"The pleasure of doing good is the only one that never wears out."*
Primitive Magic and Old Customs — Mrs. Pellew, Arlesey House.
Competition — Home-made Toffee, to be sold for funds.
Entertainment — Odsey Women's Institute Members.

March 15th.—*"No one is useless in this world who lightens the burden for anyone else."*
Talk by Mrs. Wilkinson—Group Leader.
Competition—Felt Slippers.
Entertainment—Mr. Witts' Concert Party.

April 19th.—Open Meeting.—*"Nothing lovelier can be found in woman, than to study household good."*
Cookery Demonstration—Messrs. Brown & Polsons.
Competition—Best Artificial Posy.
Entertainment—Short Concert.

May 17th.—*"Success is the compensation for concentrated endeavour."*
Song Lecture on Old English Ballads, Miss I. E. Clear, Bassingbourn.
Competition—Cookery.
Entertainment - Sketch by Members.

May 24th.—*"Footprints on the sand of time are not made by sitting down."*
Ashwell Women's Institute 10th Birthday Party.

June 21st.—Open Meeting.—*"Cheerfulness will oil toil."*
Handwork Demonstration, Trays, Mr. R. R. Bunn, St. Albans.
Competition—Guessing Parcel by feeling it.
Entertainment — Dancing by Ashwell Morris Team.

July—Outing— *"If your face wants to smile—let it: If it doesn't—make it."*

August—*"Above the clouds the skies are blue."*
Picnic.

Sept. 20th.—Open Meeting.—*"Not having any faults is a great fault indeed."*
Reminiscences of Bethnal Green — Rev. H. R. Humphreys, Therfield.
Competition—
Entertainment—Musical.

Oct. 18th—*"A great deal of talent is lost to the world for want of a little courage."*
Members' Evening.
Nominations for New Committee.

Nov. 15th.—*"The self-depreciation that is a cloak for shirking responsibility is not the kind of meekness that shall inherit the earth."*
Annual Business Meeting.
Election of Officers and Committee. Reports.
Talk on Women Police.

Dec. 13th.—(2nd Thursday),—*"A merry heart killeth more microbes than any medicine."*
Christmas Party.

Meetings will be held in Ashwell Village Hall, on 3rd Thursdays, unless otherwise stated, at 7 p.m.
Annual Membership Fee 2/-. Refreshments by Tea Hostesses.

Herts Federation Meetings—Spring Meeting, Hitchin, March 31st. Musical Festival, W.I. Day, April 25th, Haileybury College, Hertford. Annual Meeting, St. Albans, October 17th.
National Federation Meetings—London, May 22nd and 23rd.

WOMEN'S LAND ARMY.

CERTIFICATE OF DISCHARGE ON DEMOBILISATION.

Name Butt, Alice Mary
Enrolled on 25.4.17 at Hitchin
Demobilised on 30.11.19 at Hertford
Special remarks as to Qualifications and Awards
Good Service Ribbon

Her work during her period of Service in the Women's Land Army has been
Excellent
Her personal character has been
Excellent
D. Stone
(Signature of County Organising Secretary.)
Date 16.12.19 County Herts.

Right: *Alice Butt*
Alice later married Roland Worboys and they lived for many years in Chain Cottages.

A Fordham letterheading

E. K. & H. FORDHAM, LIMITED.

TELEGRAPH OFFICE AND STATION ASHWELL.
TELEPHONE Nº 2 ASHWELL.
TELEGRAMS: ASHWELL HERTS.

LONDON OFFICES AND STORES
HARRINGAY STATION, G.N.R.
NEAR FINSBURY PARK, N.4.

ASHWELL BREWERY, NEAR BALDOCK, HERTS. Oct 21st 1922

STATEMENT OF THE ASHWELL CHURCH ACCOUNTS

For Year ending Easter, 1914.

Receipts.

		£	s.	d.
	CHURCH COLLECTIONS.			
	From March 30th, 1913, to April 12th, 1914 ...	50	17	11
	SUBSCRIPTIONS.			
1914.	Balance in hand	6	13	1
Feb. 6.	Mrs. Timms	0	5	0
„ 12.	Mr. Bacon	1	10	0
Mar. 23.	Mr. E. Snow Fordham	1	0	0
„ 23.	Mr. W. A. Fordham	3	0	0
„ 23.	Mr. Gamble	1	1	0
„ 24.	Mrs. Spencer	0	10	0
„ 24.	Mrs. Bowman	1	0	0
„ 24.	Mr. W. H. Bayliss	0	10	6
„ 26.	Mr. E. Anderson	0	10	6
„ 28.	Mr. W. Cooper	1	0	0
„ 28.	Mrs. Huggins	0	5	0
„ 29.	Mr. J. W. Pack...	1	0	0
April 4.	Mr. J. Kingsley...	0	10	6
„ 4.	Mrs. Walkden	0	10	0
„ 5.	Messrs. B. & A. Christy	1	0	0
„ 6.	Mrs. Sale	0	12	0
„ 6.	Mr. and Mrs. Goble	1	0	0
„ 9.	Mrs. Wallace	0	5	0
„ 9.	Mrs. Stewart Weigall	0	10	0
„ 14.	Mr. J. Page	1	1	0
„ 16.	Messrs. A. & C. Christy	0	10	6
June 6.	Messrs, J. & H. Christy	0	10	0
„ 6.	Mr. S. Parkhouse	0	10	0
„ 6.	J. Sale	1	0	0
July 16.	Mr. R. Hine	0	10	6
		77	12	6
July 6.	Sale of two old stoves to Mr. J. W. Pack	2	0	0
		79	12	6
	Balance due to Churchwardens at Easter, 1914	9	3	3
		£88	15	9

Expenditure.

		£	s.	d.
1913.	Expenses attending Visitation ...	1	0	0
May 28.	J. Picking, Sweeping Church Walls, &c.	0	4	0
„ 28.	Ashwell Saddlery Co., Mending Ropes	0	5	4
„ 30.	H. Picking, Repairing and Painting Fence to Churchyard	3	18	0
„ 31.	Mrs. Burr, Cleaning Church ...	1	10	0
June 19.	Ecclesiastical Insurance (Accident)	0	10	0
July 7.	London Assurance (Fire)... ...	3	16	6
„ 18.	Mrs. Picking, Washing Surplices ...	0	9	0
Oct. 8.	Mrs. Picking, Washing Surplices ...	0	9	0
„ 15.	Messrs. Warren Bros., Printing ...	0	13	6
„ 18.	Mrs. Picking, Washing and Repairing Surplices	0	11	6
„ 27.	J. Picking, Putting up Chiming Ropes	0	3	0
1914.				
Jan. 16.	Faculty (for Church Warming Apparatus)	2	2	0
Feb. 3.	A. J. Hoye, Repairing Windows ...	1	5	0
Mar. 12.	Cheque Book	0	2	6
„ 12.	F. J. Bailey & Co., Repairing Small Tower over Porch	14	10	0
April 4.	S. Picking, repairing floor behind organ	1	4	9
„ 6.	H. Picking, repairing two doors ...	0	3	6
„ 11.	Mrs. Picking, washing surplices, &c.	0	10	9
„ 16.	Messrs. A & C. Christy, coal account	10	4	3
„ 23.	J. G. Clark, 1 year's salary ...	10	0	0
June 6.	Messrs. J. & H. Christy, candles, oil, &c.	6	13	9
„ 23.	Mr. A. W. Chote, 1 year's salary ...	15	0	0
July 6.	Messrs. J. W. Pack & Son, green paint for fence to Churchyard	1	5	0
„ 14.	H. Pack, attending to heating apparatus	2	10	0
„ 14.	Mrs. Burr, 1 year's dusting ...	4	0	0
„ 14.	J. Picking, 1 year's chiming ...	2	12	0
„ 14.	W. Waldock, 1 year's organ blowing	2	12	0
„ 14.	Mrs. Burr, insurance stamps ...	0	10	5
		£88	15	9

BENJAMIN CHRISTY,
JOHN W. SALE, } *Churchwardens.*

I hereby certify that I have examined these accounts for the past year and find them correct,

JAMES W. PACK.

Ashwell Church Accounts for 1914.
Note W.Waldock paid £2.12.0 for 1 years organ blowing.
(Museum)

The Rev S.W.P. Webb,
Rector of Ashwell 1892-1925
(The author)

A Kaleidoscope of Characters

The village was not dominated by an aristocratic family. Mrs Phyllis Fordham, the sort of "squiress", was very well known both in Ashwell and in the county. Quite often misunderstood and some would say difficult, she always put Ashwell first. Mr Wolverley Fordham, her husband, had died in 1921, aged 62, leaving her with about a thousand acres of land, farms, houses, buildings and cottages. She was then living at Redlands Grange. Her home, Ashwell Bury, which had been used as a military hospital during the war, was remodelled by Sir Edwyn Lutyens, a famous architect, early in the twenties, over a period of three years.

Mrs Fordham was extremely active in village affairs and outside -churchwarden, parish, rural and county councillor, Girl Guide Commissioner, (although she insisted on pronouncing it "Gal" Guide) and with the Nursing Association. In fact, she was connected with every committee in the parish. The local Liberal Party, which all the Fordhams had supported, was known to hold rallies in the Bury grounds. She died in 1958 aged 76.

Sir Herbert George Fordham, although resident at Odsey, spent much of his time at Ashwell, where he was chairman of the family firm of brewers, until his death in 1929. Among his many activities he was a Unitarian, barrister, cartographer and like his ancestors a Liberal, standing for Parliament on at least one occasion. An article, complete with cartoon of Sir George brandishing a revolver, appeared in the Hitchin Conservative & Unionist Gazette dated 11th February 1911. Apparently Sir George was speaking at an open air meeting of the Liberal party at Therfield, when boys threw mud at him and he rather unwisely drew a revolver.

He was also a Cambridgeshire county councillor, and at one time Deputy Lieutenant for that county. He was buried in the Odsey mausoleum with his two wives.

George Russell Blake Fordham, a son of Sir Herbert George Fordham, was sent to Ashwell to learn the art of brewing, in the days when Ashwell barley, Ashwell water and Kentish hops made real beer. It was necessary for him to reside at one of the firm's inns, the Bushel and Strike, so that with the resident brewer he could inspect all stages of the brewing process, even during the night.

Russell fell in love with the Bushel's barmaid. It is said that he was cut off without even a shilling. The couple married and emigrated to Canada, where Russell worked at all sorts of jobs, fruit farming, demolition and concrete work. Eventually, with his wife and two daughters he returned to live in a cottage at Steeple Morden, employed as a building worker by F.J. Bailey & Co. An old bricklayer friend of mine told me that whilst building some council houses at Therfield, the foreman pointed out a bulge in one outer wall. Russell quickly replied, "They will have to set a rose bush to hide it".

Russell was a good cricketer, although not always abiding by the rules. There is the story told of a bowler calling "How's that!" The umpire asked, "Who is it?" When told, "Mr Fordham", he replied, "Not out". Russell Fordham later became a director of the brewery.

These lines appeared in the "Herts and Cambs Reporter" of Friday 18th February 1966:

FORDHAM - In memory of my elder brother Russell Fordham Esq., J.P. of Odsey and his wife, and of my great friend Mrs Addison (nee Worthington).

No gun shall sound. No beaters thresh
And no hounds hunt in the hedges
On my land of Next Odsey till February 1st 1967 -
The peace of the dead.
Red is the colour of human love
Like the deep red scented roses.
So I brought him deep red roses
As my farewell gift to him
And I laid them on his coffin
For all the world to see.
And for my friend
Hast thou the key?
There is a little postern door
If thy key fits open and enter.
There is mystery beyond that door
The mystery of life and death and peace.

by Marjory C Fordham of Odsey. The Hertfordshire Poet.

William Herbert Fordham, another son of Sir George, was born in 1883, trained as a civil engineer, and worked at the Thames Iron Works on the first Thunderer which was launched in 1911. From 1914 he worked abroad as a consulting oil engineer, a profession which he found very exciting and for which he was awarded the Redwood medal for services to petroleum in 1929, the year his father died. With regret he gave up his extremely promising career in oil in exchange for beer.

In 1929 Willie Herbert, as he was known, came back and settled at Odsey, the family home, to manage the brewery until its closure in 1965. At the same time he became interested in public work, representing Ashwell on Hitchin Rural District Council, was chairman of Letchworth Naturalists' Association and a trustee of Ashwell Museum.

An interesting item appeared in one of the daily newspapers dated 11 September 1912. "Foreigners and English girls. Thrashing and fine for insult." "In this country, women are able to walk about without being molested by young blackguards", declared Mr Edward Snow Fordham, the magistrate at West London police court, yesterday. Miss McGarry stated that as she passed Ricardo Bachi, an Italian student aged 21, on the pavement, he touched her under the chin. Mr McGarry, the father, thrashed the student, injuring his leg.

Imposing on the student a fine of 40s. with 7s. 6d. doctor's fee, Mr Fordham said, "We have too many foreigners in this country. Keep your filthy tricks for the country you came from. If the law allowed, I should order you to be flogged as a lesson to you and a warning to others."

E.K. & O. Fordham had been brewers in Mill Street since the early 1800s. In 1832 they bought the plant, including the 50 gallon vat, off Mr Porter who had been brewing at the corner of Mill Street and Carters pond. Later, after the early death of Oswald Fordham, Herbert George Fordham joined the firm and it became E.K. & H. Fordham and remained so until its takeover by Greens of Luton and soon afterwards by Whitbreads. It closed and was demolished in 1973. Today only the offices, the stable block and the maltings remain, all converted into dwellings, and along by the river, a few houses have been built in what is called Fordham Close.

The firm was flourishing in the 1920s and 1930s when it was being run by four Fordham brothers, producing a range of ales, beers and stout, supplied in bottle or barrel and delivered to its many pubs and hotels over a wide area. Mild beer sold at fourpence a pint, straight from the barrel: pumps and tubes were then only just being introduced. The firm's transport consisted of two Foden steam wagons and a fleet of petrol lorries. In addition, Fordhams owned a London depot at Harringay. The beers were sent to the depot by rail from Ashwell station and then delivered to London clubs and hotels by the firm's men and lorries stationed at Harringay.

Mrs Amy Critchley, a sister of Mr W.A. Fordham, lived at Redlands Grange in the mid-twenties after her sister-in law moved back into the Bury. Rita Critchley, her daughter, joined the Roman Catholic church, she organised the few local faithful and had services arranged at the village hall. On one occasion, she remarked that one must reside in Ashwell for thirty years before being recognised as an Ashwellian. Rita Critchley went out to do missionary work in Africa and was murdered by the Mau Mau in Kenya. One of her cousins said that he was not in the least surprised, because she probably tried to boss the Africans in the same way that she did people here!

During the 18th century, doctors named Kintish, Savage, Webster, Barnby, Ellard, Nunn and Hix were called in from Royston, Baldock, Potton and Hertford. In 1819, Dr Hicks from Baldock agreed with the "Gentlemen of Ashwell" to attend the poor for £22 yearly. Dr Charles Woodforde became Ashwell's first resident doctor in 1820. It is said that he went to India where he was eaten by a tiger. Dr Laroux came in 1829 followed by Dr Tyndale in 1829.

Old Ashwell people remember Dr R.E.H. Woodforde, one of whose distant ancestors was Parson Woodforde of diary fame. Dr Woodforde came to Ashwell in 1900 and was on call to his many patients in the village and the surrounding villages seven days a week, which often meant driving out in the pony and trap in the early hours. He was Ashwell's first car owner - a De Dion Bouton. Later he went over to cars made by Henry Ford and, for short distances, used a motor cycle or bicycle. A paragraph in the "Royston Crow" of July 1933 describes Dr Woodforde's retirement and quotes him as saying "Dr Tyndale had to deal with such dread diseases as smallpox and typhoid and on one occasion said, 'The Mordens will kill me'. I must confess to the same feelings at times, but I am sure he was as sad at leaving them as I am today".

Doctor John Moynihan and his wife, Doctor Sheila, followed Dr. Woodforde and their son, Doctor Fergus Moynihan, carries on the practice today, together with his three partners, in a purpose-built Health Centre in Gardiners Lane.

The Woodfordes had one daughter, Dorothy, and four sons. Jack, an engineer, worked on the erection of Wallington radio masts. Alex became a doctor. Christopher was at one time vicar of Steeple Morden; he also held livings at Exford and Axbridge, Somerset; then became chaplain of New College, Oxford and lastly Dean of Wells until he died at the age of 49. An authority on stained glass, Christopher wrote two books on the subject and guides to several famous churches. He held a doctorate of both Oxford and Cambridge.

Oliver, the youngest son, studied law, served in North Africa and Italy and as a major in the Royal Corps of Signals, was mentioned in despatches and awarded the

Lesley Worboys lost a leg in World War I. Trained as a boot & shoe repairer and ran a small repair shop next to the Rose & Crown. (Museum)

Two sons of Baker Leopold Day. Left, Charles Day – father of Howard Day. Right, Edward Day – ran a Bakers business in Nottingham (I believe). (Museum)

William Picking, World War I. Later employed by F.J. Bailey in the Sawmills. William was a son of Walter Picking of the old firm of Walt. Sam and Herb. Pickings Carpenters & Undertakes, who reroofed the nave of Ashwell Church last century placing the huge timbers over the nave.. (Museum)

Kenneth Bryant R.A.M.C., World War I. Son of Butcher Bryant later Crumps. Kenneth played the piano for the silent films at the Village hall in the 1920s. Joined the R.A.F. in World War II. (Museum)

Frank Sheldrick, Royal Artillery, World War I. Later gardener at Ashwell Bury, then in charge of Ashwell's Water supply. (Museum)

Albert Covington, World War I. Later manager of J.H. Christy's Grocers shop. Later still became landlord of the Engine pub in Back Street. (Museum)

George Moss (1824-1909), an Ashwell boy who made good. Built the Moss Cottage Homes. (Museum)

Silas Worboys, Wheelwright and Wesleyan local preacher at the doorway of his wheelwrights shop, c.1930. (Museum)

Visit of Merchant Taylors Company Officials, early 1920s in the Rectory Garden.
Left to right: *Mrs Phyllis Fordham, Mrs J. Sale, Rev S.P. Webb, Mrs P. Wilson, Mrs Talbot, Mrs Webb, 3 Merchant Taylors, Miss Cooper, J. Sale, W. Wilson, 3 Merchant Taylors, W. Cooper.*
(Museum)

Mrs Wolverley Fordham with Dr John Moynihan on the left. She was very averse to being photographed, and this one has been enlarged by 160%. (Mrs Berry)

Clive Whitby – one of Ashwell's best known characters. Now 81, worked for many years at Westbury farm. Verger at the Parish Church from 1978 to the present day. (Museum)

Our excuse for including this picture is that it is a group of people mostly born in Ashwell. Most have passed away, but no one has been able to identify the occasion. (The Comet newspaper)

Florence Worboys (1896-1987). Ashwell's Postlady for over 60 years. Retired at the age of 87 in 1983. Flo was awarded the B.E.M. in the 1982 Birthday Honours List.
(Museum)

Ashwell's 'Three Wise Men', William Holloway, Jim Davies and Percy Dellar, c.1930. The three men walked round the village every day.
(Howard Day)

A Wesleyan Methodist group taken in the back yard of their Chapel about 1930.
Front Row, left to right: *Alice Waldock, Mrs Alf Brown & daughter, Mrs Arthur Harradine, Mrs Amy Parrish, Mrs C. Miller, Mrs Owen Waldock, Mrs Eley, Silas Worboys, Gwen Page, Mrs Ralph Covington, Phyllis Bullard, Mrs Albert Hall & daughter, Mrs Cheetham, Mrs Knight.*
Second Row: *Mrs W. White, Mrs E. Searle, Mrs M. Kirchin, Emma Edwards, Mrs Edwards, Mrs Ben Bryant, Mrs Huffer, Mrs Hollingsworth, -----?, Mrs A. Bullard, Mrs Charles Worboys, Mr C. Worboys.*
Third Row: *Ben Bryant, -----?, Mrs Fred Gentle, Mrs Fred Page, Miss Bryant, Miss Irene Worboys, Miss Bryant, Doris Brown, Mrs Brown, Mrs E. Brown, Mrs Stanley Bryant, Olive Covington, -----?, Miriam Huffer, -----?, Mrs W. Harvey.*
Fourth Row: *Mrs S. Jarman, Alf Brown & daughter, -----?, Mrs Ball, Eric Gilbert, Fred Page, George Page, Peter Skerman, Stan Jarman, Rene Page, Charles Page, Jock Skerman, Ralph Covington, Mrs Bill Waldock, Amos Covington, Mrs Ernest Picking, Miss Huffer, Charles Brown, Miss Hyslop, Mrs Albert Skerman, Charles Miller, Albert Skerman.*
Background: *Over the wall Bill Robinson's orchard (Bulls Head). Right Methodist toilets.*

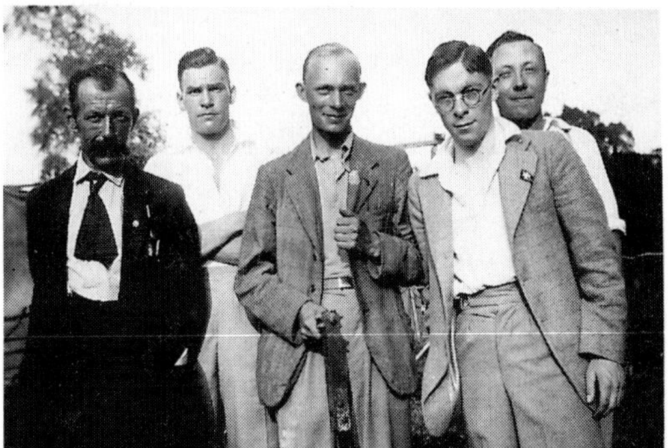

Above: *TOC H helpers at the 1937 Ashwell Show. Left to right: Albert Skerman, Eric Harradine, Albert Sheldrick, John Bray, Stanley Andrews.* (The author)

Left: *An Ashwell group take it easy in their Sunday best, c.1925.*
Front: *Stanley Brown, Stanley Bryant, "Coffee" Clements.*
Second Row: *Frank Gentle, Joe Capon, Ted Ball.*
Back Row: *Don Bryant, -----?, -----?.* (The author)

The Ashwell Branch of the Ancient Order of Foresters: Members of the band in front of the club's banner, c.1910. (Museum)

Above: *Ashwell's oldest resident in 1991 – 98 years old Mrs E. Webb. Educated at the Board Schools, at 13 she went into service in the household of Mr W.H. Bayliss, Fordham's Brewer and later, Mrs Woodforde's parents in London. She married in the 1st World War; her husband Ernie worked for Mrs Fordham.* (Ian Walters)

Above right: *Ashwell's oldest man in 1991 – Bill Hardyman, at 95 still painting.*

Right: *Bill in 1898 – second from the left. Note the Designer clothes!* (W. Hardyman)

Ashwell Men's Club Annual Dinner, 1927. (Howes family)
Standing: *5 ladies, Morgan Biles, Ben Christy, W.A. Appleton, John Sale, Rev Henry Griffith, J.R. Burton, Alfred Angell, -----?, W. Wylie, Henry Bonnett.*
Solitary standing figure: *George Holloway*
Seated (from left): *Neville Howes, Gersham Wylie, Oscar Burgess, Tommy Dennis, Derek Kearney, Edward Wilkins, Hubert Radford, Hector Pammenter, Fred Albon, 4 not recognised, Albert Huffer, Alan Smith.*
Seated (from right): *Albert Harradine, Don Bryant, Stan Bryant, -----?, Stan Edwards, Jack (Turkey) Worboys, Bob Reynolds, Noah Geeves, Jack Oyston, Len Bullimore, H. Bonness, Mark Crump, Charles Westrope, Ken Bryant.*

British Legion Dinner, 1950s
Top table: *Mark Crump (Chairman),-----?, -----?, W.H. Fordham, Rev Jack Catterick, -----?, A. Farr, D.S. Sheppard.*
Table on left:
Outer: *W. Whitehead, S. Whitehead, Mr & Mrs B. Hankin, Mrs V. Izzard, Mr & Mrs W. Revel, B. Hankin (Junior), Mr S. Revil, E. Eversden, K. Revil, R. Rosendale, George Turner, Tommy Dennis.*
Inner: *R. Skerman, W. Barton, D. Kingsley, B. Simmonds, P. Crump, T. Wylie, -----?, -----?, S. Reynolds, Mr Worboys, W. James, L. Gallant, -----?, -----?, H. Day.*
Table on right:
Inner: *Mr & Mrs F. Pettengell, Mrs Andrews, G. Chapman, Ian Picking, S. Cherry, R. White, L. Bryant, -----?, J. Worboys, S. Picking, T. Dodson, -----?, -----?, Mrs L. Bryant, A. Sheldrick, -----?, -----?.*
Outer: *Mr & Mrs S. Worboys, Mrs G. Foster, Mr & Mrs B. Seaby, Mrs & Mr Collins, -----?, Miss G. Haylock, Mrs Griffiths, Mrs Harradine, Mrs Ward, Mrs Livings, -----?, W. Sale, Mrs & Mr Glover.*

The old school in Ashwell

THIS photograph was taken half a century ago, but I remember the occasion well.

It depicts Standard III (ten-year-olds) of Ashwell Primary School, and was taken in the playground, against the fence of the School House, where the then headmistress, Miss Annie Hyslop, lived.

Also on the staff were Miss Annie Bray and Miss Street.

Back row, left to right: Fred Ward, Doreen Hall, Geoff Picking, Molly Smith, ? Walker.

Middle row, left to right: Leon Picking, Pearl Glasscock, Norman Gurney, Kathleen Law, Ray Skerman.

Front row, left to right: Tony Eley, Eileen Brown, Ena Cook, John Anderson.

(Mrs) PEARL WILLIAMS
(nee Glasscock)

17 Letchworth Road
Stevenage

A very important event, when in 1973 Whitbreads hand over the Springs to Ashwell Parish. Pictured: *Councillors P. Milton, Eric Gurney, Howard Day, Jeremy Fordham, Sam Wallace, Dr Fergus Moynihan, Gurney Sheppard, Philip Crump, John Bray and William H. Fordham; Solicitor Geoffrey Coad and representatives of Whitbread's Brewery.* (Museum)

The Foundation Stone laying ceremony of the Moss Cottage Home s in Hodwell in 1904. Top-hatted George Moss addressing the crowd, is just left of centre of the picture. (Museum)

M.B.E. After the war he became the official solicitor to the Church Commissioners and legal adviser to the General Synod of the Church of England. Shortly before he retired, Oliver was honoured by the Queen with the C.B.E.

Mrs Noyes, who lived at Ringstead, seemed a rather strange woman to me. Perhaps it was because she used to breed Shetland ponies, and walk them through the village.

Miss Pearce, another strange woman, lived at Partridge Hall with a few goats. One of twelve children, my uncle, Percy Sheldrick, was befriended by Miss Pearce. While he was still a schoolboy, she taught him the art of embroidery. There are a few of his little pictures still around. At the age of eighteen he exhibited an embroidered banner entitled "The Good Shepherd" at a London exhibition and was awarded a certificate of merit.

Percy joined the Beds & Herts regiment at the outbreak of war and was severely wounded in France. After his discharge from the forces, he was given the opportunity to learn the art of tapestry weaving as carried out at the Gobelin works in France. Then followed two years of study at the London School of Arts & Crafts. He was then offered a post as a weaver at the William Morris tapestry works at Merton Abbey. Here for eighteen years he worked as a master weaver, where his first work was "The Passing of Venus" from a design by Sir Edward Burne Jones. The piece, 9 feet by 20 feet, took three and a half years to complete; it now hangs in the Detroit Institute of Arts, U.S.A.

Two panels of the Holy Grail series hang above the altar of Lancing College chapel. The city coat of arms hanging in St Mary's Hall, Coventry, is also by Percy Sheldrick. The Morris works closed in 1939. Percy continued working from his home and his banners and a triptych in gold thread can be seen in Ashwell church; "St Vincent" at Newnham church in memory of Reginald L Hine, the Hitchin historian; other pieces of his work are at Baldock church, where his mother was born, and at Thriplow church, Cambridgeshire, where his father was born, and a sampler in Ashwell museum.

When Mrs Phyllis Fordham developed her Bluegates dairy in High Street, she imported some young men with a knowledge of dairy work. One came from Dorset, another from Sussex and young Neville Howes from Coventry, who was in charge of the bottling, cream separation and the milk round, seven days a week.

At that time the milk was delivered by a horse-drawn float, in a large churn with a brass tap; it was run off into an oval bucket with a hinged lid, which the roundsman carried from door to door, along with a pint and a half-pint measure to fill the customer's jugs. There were often times when the horse was difficult. I remember when it took fright and dashed off as far as Hinxworth with Neville, using extremely strong language, in hot pursuit. It was with great relief that eventually he took charge of an electric van.

Neville Howes raised three sons, and in his very limited spare time became one of Ashwell's keenest voluntary workers. When the Howes came to live in the converted brewery office at the entrance to the former Page's brewery, the village had just bought the old malting at the end of the yard, and was trying to raise the money to convert it into a village hall with adjoining Men's Social Club.

Neville devoted his every spare moment to this cause, selling draw tickets, helping to organise all kinds of events and even when the hall was completed in 1922, he was the volunteer who kept the boiler stoked up to keep the premises heated and able to supply the hot water for the sixpenny baths. He was to the fore in the Ashwell Choral and Dramatic Society, and in the Men's Club. When war came again, he joined the Observer Corps and after the war ended it was his idea to form the Ashwell Film Society.

Mrs Josiah Worboys and Mrs Liza Winters (known as Liza Durgins) achieved fame in the days of straw plaiting, that is until the early years of this century. Both lived in the row of cottages then known as Workhouse Row, and were still there well into the 1920s. The workhouse was the taller section of the row, nearest to Gardiners Lane.

The two women were experts at straw plaiting, and on one occasion argued as to who was the faster. Eventually they were persuaded to take their bundles of straws up to the top of the church tower, some 150 feet high, and plait away over the side until one or the other's straw plait touched the ground, at the base of the tower. Unfortunately, like so many village tit-bits, no one bothered to record the winner!

Most of the village people had nicknames in those days, usually as a means of identification. There was Joey "Longbeard" Waldock, to identify him from all the other Waldocks, Levy, Sam and Bill, and Jimmy "Bunny" Waldock who stuttered. Then there were the dozens of Worboys. To name just a few: Sam, Silas, Bill, Jimmy "Tight" Worboys, Jack "Turkey" Worboys, Ernest "Brassy" Worboys, and the most famous or some would same infamous, Arthur "Shaver" Worboys.

The last named, a big strong man, a Mons hero, worked as a navvy on the building of the Wembley Exhibition in the early 1920s. "Shaver" wandered all over the country, working here and there, drinking heavily, and returning to his mother's cottage in Silver Street from time to time, borrowing half a crown here and a shilling there, which he would repay months afterwards. I often wondered why some folks spoke of Mrs Charley "Brown" Wilkins, until I discovered that her first husband's surname was Brown and her second was Wilkins, and it was the same with Mrs "Brown" Crack.

"Clicker" Burr, a quiet, civil little man, worked at Dixies farm and lodged at the Engine. Joe Toft, a dwarfish little man and hot tempered, was for some years the lime burner at the Hinxworth road lime kiln. Caleb Saunders, a smiling bearded man, looked after the cattle housed in buildings known as "The Pump". When young, Caleb was frightened by the lightning which struck an old building in Bennetts lane. For ever after, at the merest hint of a thunderstorm, Caleb would run and hide himself in the nearest strawstack.

Peter Skerman, also bearded, rather fiercer than Caleb, was unable to read or write. For a good many years, he was the limeburner for F.J. Bailey & Co, and when Dr Woodforde told him that the little sharp, black, thorn-like objects he pecked out of the chalk were actually the teeth of prehistoric sharks, Peter was on to a good thing. Peter's drinking place was the Rose & Crown, and here he would approach any stranger who looked good for a pint. Quite soon a fossil shark's tooth would change hands for a fourpenny pint of Simpsons mild beer.

Rufus and Ben Bonfield, two bachelor brothers - it was said that Rufus was married for a short time - lived with their mother on Ashwell Street near the Pest House. Rufus was a carpenter and Ben a painter. Both were employed by John Bailey, the Ashwell builder, who was, I understand, their cousin. Both were extremely fond of the bottle and on one occasion Ben, with two other painters, was decorating the main bedroom at Ashwell Bury. At lunch time, Ben just happened to drop in at The Bushel & Strike for a glass of ale to wash down his sandwiches. Here he met some old drinking friends, with the result that when he was able to stagger back to the bedroom, the two painters found that he was helpless and decided to put him to bed. So Ben slept the afternoon away in the four poster bed. Fortunately for Ben, Mrs Fordham had made her inspection of the decorations in the morning.

In their spare time the two little brothers - neither was more than five feet tall - tended their large garden and a number of beehives. Mainly at weekends, they sold cut flowers at sixpence a bunch and honey at a shilling a pound.

Then there was the little spinster, Emma Edwards, who lived in one of the Silver Street cottages: a simple old soul, very fond of children. When a group called out "Dance, Emma" she would lift up her ankle-length skirt and perform a little jig, at the same time singing a song in the middle of the street.

Farms and Fields

According to the book, Ashwell is a parish of 4,108 acres. Agriculture is, and always was, the principal industry. Apart from wheat, barley, oats, potatoes, peas, brussels sprouts and beans, mangel wurzels and swede turnips were also grown, stored in pits or clamps, covered with straw and earth to be used as cattle feed in winter. Then there were the hay crops of clover, trefoil, lucerne and sainfoin. Occasionally, there would be a field of the beautiful pale blue linseed. The Ashwell pronunciation was wozzels, tunnups and trayfile. Until well into the twenties ploughing, rolling, harrowing, drilling, hoeing, reaping and harvesting were all done by men and horses.

For a few years steam ploughing was popular, especially on heavy land. A steam traction engine was positioned at either end of a field. Below each engine, a large drum was fixed containing a roll of heavy steel cable, the end of which was attached to a wide, heavy steel double plough. The plough, with a man seated on it, was drawn across the field to the first engine, then the plough was reversed so that the plough could be drawn back to the second engine and so on until the ploughing was completed.

Gordon Cooper of Ashwell, the Kendalls of Millow, Bedfordshire, and William Hunt of Steeple Morden, Cambridgeshire, all undertook this work. It was an expensive operation. Apart from the two engine drivers and the man on the plough, and the oiling, greasing and maintenance of the machines, there had to be a back-up service for the supply of coal and water to keep the engines working, sometimes late into the night. When fresh supplies were needed we would hear a blast on the engine's whistle demanding more coal or water, and if kept waiting it was a long angry blast.

Apart from the arable side of Ashwell's farms and the milk producers, most of the farmers raised beef cattle in the meadow close to the farmhouse and pigs and chickens in one of the yards behind the farmhouse, and of course there were two or three heavy horses to each hundred acres of land.

Earlier in the century there was a flock of sheep on each farm. I was puzzled by the name given to a yard at Westbury farm (the old men spoke of it as the "ship yard") until I learned that sheep used to be driven in there in the winter. In the twenties, there were only two flocks of sheep in Ashwell - shepherd Crack in charge of the Bluegates flock and Tommy Potton the Whitby farm flock.

Farrows Farm at West End was part of a large estate owned by J.T. Mills, a Norfolk banker, and has been in the occupation of the Sale family for generations. John Sale bought the farm in 1918. The land stretches over the peak of Newnham Hill on both sides of the road, down to Newnham Bottom and then on again to the parish boundary. It is a light chalky soil, which certainly shows during a dry spell after deep ploughing.

Some of Ashwell's older inhabitants will remember John Sale's tribute to the "Daily Mail's" weather forecasts for farmers during the twenties. On the gentle slope of Ash hill, the field which stretches from the western side of Arbury Banks towards the Newnham boundary, each letter of the message "THANK YOU DAILY MAIL" was measured out carefully. Mustard seed was then sown to form the huge letters, and as the green message grew, more mustard seed was sown over the rest of the field, and eventually the golden "THANK YOU DAILY MAIL" stood out boldly in a field of green. There is a photograph at Ashwell museum of Mr Sale standing by his Wolseley car looking across from Newnham Bottom at his work of art.

Mr Sale was a good farmer. I believe it was he who introduced the tractor to Ashwell. A regular churchman, he believed in "six days shalt thou labour" and when friends complained about the weather, he would quote "Seedtime and harvest shall not fail". When in his eighties, I remember Mr Sale telling me that his television set was his best buy. He lived to a good age and was succeeded at Farrows farm by his grandson, Sam Wallace.

The Christy family occupied **Westbury Farm** from the 17th century and were always connected with the church as churchwardens, or were overseers of the poor, but it seems that on a few occasions they may have strayed away from the fold. During the second half of the 18th century it is possible that they dabbled in Methodism, because it is on record that John Berridge, the great Calvinistic parson from Everton, Bedfordshire, held a number of services in a barn at Westbury farm.

Recently it has been written that John Bunyan preached at Westbury farm. There is no evidence of this but it is recorded that he 'preached in a barn belonging to Ann Christy "in the middle of the town"'. At one time the Christys had leanings towards the Society of Friends. Westbury farm was also part of the banker Mills estate, and was purchased by Benjamin Christy in 1918. The land lay alongside that of Farrows farm only separated by the bridleway to Caldecote. It consisted mainly of one huge 200-acre wedge-shaped field, following the bridleway over Quarry Hill down to "Carcote" bottom, hitting the Ashwell-Hinxworth road at the Cuckoo pub. Back towards Ashwell it takes in the ancient chalk quarries where for centuries blocks of clunch stone were hewn, and the lime kiln where the lime was burnt to make mortar to build not only Ashwell but many of the churches in the area. Finally the road goes on to Westpoint, the thin end of the wedge, a farm gate wide.

The 16th century Westbury farm house was built inside a moat which it is believed was originally dug to surround an eleventh century manor house. There is a smaller moat to the west of the original moat. It surrounds a long, narrow island, where at the turn of the century there were boating and bathing parties. This was a very pleasant spot.

At the south-west corner of the moat, a spring of clear water (the only water supply for the Iron Age villagers at Arbury Banks) collected in a pool before flowing through a sluice gate and forming a miniature waterfall to fill the moat, then on again through a second and third sluice before tumbling into a wide ditch known as the Watercress ditch. Good quality watercress was cultivated here until the farm house sewer outfall seeped into the moat.

The small fields nearby had such lovely names as Willow Bit, Cow Drift and Edwards Eye. The ditch itself goes wandering on its way to join the river Cam, linking up with other ditches and land drains, past Buttway cottages, skirting the road towards Ashwell End, to join the little river Rhee running from Ashwell Springs to Cambridge.

I have wandered away from the village to point out that before 1939 the water levels of Ashwell's springs, wells, ponds, ditches and streams were much higher than now. As a schoolboy, by simply winding up the Westbury sluice I caused the road to be flooded from Buttway cottages almost to Ashwell End! Today that spring is almost dried up. And the Christys? There were four at Westbury farm, five at the village shop and eight in coal, minerals and newspapers. Today not one.

Dixies Farm House is probably of the 16th century, timber framed but covered with plaster. Over the years it has been partly burned down and altered. Its jetted gable ends with their scalloped barge boards are a feature of High Street. The lower roofed section was originally the farm brew house. The farmer, Mr William Cooper, churchman and county councillor, occupied the house with his daughter, Lilian. Immediately opposite, behind a green-painted Georgian iron fence, was Dixies orchard. Apart from a selection of apple, pear, plum and cherry trees, a patch of a rare type of Star of Bethlehem, Ornithogalum nutans, grew here. In the spring, as soon as the green leaves pushed through the grass, Mr Cooper had a circle of hurdles erected to protect the plants from the grazing cows.

The slated roofs and tarred feather-edge boarded farm buildings were behind the house, enclosing horse and cattle yards, except for one range of buildings alongside High Street, which housed the cows, their feedingstuffs and the dairy. There were double gates with iron spikes on the top in High Street, and at the far side similar gates opened into Back Street, where stood the stable block. Here the horses, the farmer and farm workers were protected from evil by a charm - a large flint stone with a natural hole in it hanging by a chain from one of the rafters. No one knew how long the charm had been in use except that it was there in 1850, when the great fire swept through Ashwell destroying all the Dixies farm buildings, and, according to the "Times" newspaper, causing £30,000 worth of damage to the village.

The present buildings were erected soon after the fire. But, with a more enlightened horsekeeper, not until a couple of years later, when glanders, a sweating disease struck down several of the horses, was the charm replaced on the advice of the horse doctor, after he had tried in vain various potions. It was rehung and stayed until the farm was mechanised and the stable became a store for artifical manure.

A century after the fire I asked the farmer, the late Maurice Brown, whether he would consider placing the charm in Ashwell museum for future generations to see. Mr Brown told me that when he first came to the farm about 1930 he asked Arthur Harradine, the old horsekeeper, to "cobweb" the rafters, throw out the old flint and limewash the stable. Arthur was horrified and told all he knew of the charm which had been passed down to him by the previous horsekeeper.

He ended by saying that if the charm was taken down by either the farmer or any of his farm workers, the good luck would be lost. Needless to say, the stable was cobwebbed and whitewashed around the charm. Mr Brown agreed that it would be safe for me to remove it to be hung in Ashwell museum where it can be seen today. An article with sketch of the flint appeared in "FolkLore", the journal of the Folk Law Society, soon after.

Today, behind the offices, shops and cottages of Dixies Development, remain the original timbers of the rebuilt farm buildings of 1850.

Dixies farm had two other unusual features. In Back Street, across the road from the stable block, was a home-made cart shed or, as it was called in Ashwell, "cart hovel". It consisted of posts let into the ground forming a rectangle. The centre post (front) bore a sign stating that "Bill Stickers Will Be Prosecuted", but it was the roof that caught the eye - just a heaped up pile of blackthorn bushes and twigs, like a bonfire, all supported on crudely cut tree branches. It appears to have kept the carts dry, which of course was its purpose. Just behind the cart hovel there was a well of good water surmounted by a cast iron pump. Before the coming of water mains this well supplied the farm and house and the cottage people living nearby.

The other feature of Dixies farm was a dovehouse, which can still be seen. It is behind the farmhouse garden; probably built in the early 18th century. Dove houses of many types have been in use in many countries for centuries; in 1850, there were between twenty and thirty in Ashwell. Their purpose was mainly to supply pigeon meat and eggs during the winter, when beef, mutton and pork (apart from salted meat) were off the menu.

In some countries, the finest melons were grown on pigeon dung. A friend of mine who lives in Norwich goes out regularly to a disused church tower to collect the droppings for his flower beds. Dixies Close, the council housing estate behind the farm, keeps alive the name of the farm meadow, which extended from Back Street up to Ashwell Street. The rest of the farm's land was off Bygrave road and over Claybush Hill, 328 feet above sea level. Here Claybush trees, two large elms, were a landmark for many miles around. Beneath was a railway sleeper seat, a pleasant spot to sit and view the countryside, or listen to the skylarks.

Like many Scotsmen, Thomas Wylie came down from Scotland at the beginning of this century with his wife, daughter Mary and sons William and Gershom. They rented **Bear Lane Farm**, now known as Bear House, which at that time was owned by Edward King Fordham of Ashwell Bury. (He gave it to his also named grandson, Edward King, who in turn left it to his brother, Oswald Fordham.) Due to low rent, the highest tithed land in Ashwell, and costly management by estate agents, the last Fordham sold it in the twenties to the Farr family of Newnham. The farmhouse is believed to have been built in the 15th century, and like most old houses has been much altered since.

It has a tiled roof and is timber framed behind the plasterwork; two oak mullioned windows and the front door frame are probably original. During alterations in 1976, the wall of one room was found to have been painted to give the appearance of wood panelling. Today it is the residence of Lindsay and Anne Colquhoun, the former being Ashwell's first resident dentist, taking over what had been Christy's Newsagent Shop in Kirby Manor.

The house was separated from Dixies farm by a pleasant garden hidden behind a wall built with blocks of clunch, the chalk stone from the Hinxworth road quarries. The farm buildings in Back Street which joined those of Dixies farm were also re-built after the fire, but not on such a grand style. Whereas the former were well planned and built of timber with slate roofs (it has been said that if all the slates were laid out on the ground they would cover an acre), the walls of the Bear Lane farm buildings were constructed of that local mixture of clay, fine chalk and chopped straw reinforced with hazel rods. The sticky ingredients were mixed together by a cart horse treading its way through the heap, after which it was poured into shuttering as concrete is today. This was known as cob walling; a good example has been preserved and can be seen in Gardiners Lane, in this case with a thatched top.

The farm buildings were roofed with pantiles probably made at Gamlingay. When the Wylies first came to Ashwell there was a flint charm in the stables. The home close in Back Street also joined Dixies Close, the remainder of the farm's land being off Kingsland Way. The Wylie family were supporters of the Congregational chapel. A very friendly man, Mr Wylie, he reminded me of the white-bearded apostles in the coloured prints of Victorian bibles. The Farm house is now known as Bear House.

As you come to a slight bend in High Street - opposite the tall Victorian block which was once Westrope's shop - there is a high grey brick wall and a house of the same grey brick. This is **Whitby Farmhouse**, which was built about 1850. The original house and buildings, including a huge dovehouse, were completely destroyed in the great fire. Mr Alfred Angell was the farmer who lived here with his wife, son and two daughters. The Angells, like most farmers, had their own pew in the parish church. The large home close was behind the farm off Silver Street. It seems to have acquired its grander name early this century.

It has been said that when Mr and Mrs John Bailey came to live in the street Mrs Bailey felt it needed upgrading and so it was unofficially given the name Silver Street. Maybe she was offended by the term used by R.L.H. at the beginning of these notes, "Old Tommy Westropes and Chapmans backsides", which of course referred to Back Street. The Whitby farm close sloped up to Ashwell Street. A public right of way runs through this meadow, known as Quakers Walk. The footpath from Silver Street passed the Friends meeting house and burial ground and ended in Ashwell Street.

The meeting house was burned down in the big fire, but the burial ground remains hidden among the 44 houses built on the meadow between 1975 and 1978. During a survey of footpaths and rights of way in the 1940s, Quakers Walk was disputed. Charles Wilkins, an old Ashwellian, put his mark to a statement that he had walked the path since his schooldays, so the path is there today.

The Whitby farm's land joins that of Farrows farm on Newnham road taking in the Iron Age earthworks known as Arbury Banks. Across to the Bygrave road it meets Dixies farm land and lower down Cat Ditch and the Bygrave boundary.

Before leaving Cat Ditch area I must mention two small farms. Pembroke farm's land joined that of Bear Lane farm on Kingsland Way and I think it carried on as far as the railway embankment. There was a small farmhouse and buildings at the bottom of the hill and a pair of farm workers' cottages further on. This farm was probably owned originally by Pembroke College, Cambridge, but in the twenties was owned by Mr Nathan Angell (father of Alfred), who lived at the house in Ashwell now known as Westpoint; he is said to have been a butcher by trade.

Hare Park Farm was a little further on. In fact, the farmhouse is on the Royston-Baldock road near the garage at Slip End. Ben Hall, the farmer, was always very smartly dressed, with breeches and highly polished boots and leggings. His main business was cattle and sheep and he attended cattle markets over a wide area, buying for the farmers in this district. On Sundays, he drove the family down in a very smart pony and trap to attend morning service at the Congregational chapel.

Henry Bowman once told me an interesting story about Hare Park farm. Ashwell was rather late in obtaining an enclosure award. The landowners and farmers were tired of the old system of half-acre strips of land divided by narrow paths or baulks, spread from one end of the parish to the other. In theory it was a very good system. Each farm, according to its acreage, had a number of strips of poor land on the chalk hills and a number of strips of better land in the northern part of the parish. In practice, much time was wasted in travelling from one part of the village to another.

A surveyor was appointed in 1857. The landowners' committee met from time to time at Ashwell Bury, the home of the squire, Edward King Fordham. Apart from the half-acre strips, there was the tricky question of Cow Common, Donkeys Common and other odd strips of land, and the common rights of many of the parishioners. The land was carefully measured and each landowner allotted the same acreage as before, except that this time it was more or less in one piece. Common rights holders were allotted small plots, and the Enclosure Award was finally granted in 1863. The surveyor asked the landowners if they agreed with his apportionment of their land. They agreed and took over their new farms, not realising that out of the paths or baulks between the half-acre strips he had pieced together a nice little farm for himself at Slip End, known as Hare Park farm!

Redlands Farm was owned by Sir Herbert George Fordham. The farmhouse, built after the enclosure award, is off the Station road. Next to the Fox Public House, now a private house, there were two or three farm workers' cottages known as the Cinques; a further pair, probably built at the same time as the farmhouse, stand next to the footpath which is not only the parish but also the county boundary between Hertfordshire and Cambridgeshire. At the top of the hill, but in Odsey parish, stands a small farmhouse built with blue Staffordshire bricks, which were probably left over when the nearby railway bridges were built in 1850. Here lived John Kingsley, Sir Herbert's farm bailiff. Mr Kingsley and Mrs Kingsley drove a smart pony and trap down to matins at Ashwell church.

When he died in 1889, Edward King Fordham left to his eldest son, Edward Snow Fordham, 1,500 acres, of which 1,000 were in Ashwell parish. He had only farmed 600 acres himself, the remainder being let to several tenants. The estate was sold by auction in 1910, when the younger brother (Wolverley Attwood Fordham) acquired about 1,000 acres. Eleven years later, in 1921, W.A. Fordham died, and the estate was left to his widow, Phyllis, along with the responsibility of 1,000 acres, and both **Bluegates and Ducklake Farms**, together with their houses, buildings and cottages.

The main part of Bluegates farmhouse was occupied by Mr Szapiro and his family, whilst the lower, cottage part of the house was let to the Bluegates stockman. Mr Szapiro was employed as the estate secretary and dealt with the business side and paperwork of the farms. The farmhouse was built mainly in the 16th century with stout oak timbers. At a later date, as housing fashions changed, it was covered with two types of plaster

Westbury Farmhouse, c.1925. (Museum)
The black building to the right of the house was originally a Dovehouse. Taken to its present position on rollers from the front meadow about 1910.

Farmer John Sale (extreme right) with his men in 1910.
(Mrs B. Wallace)

Harold Street of Hinxworth on Baileys Burrel steam engine, pulling tree trunks into Baileys Timber Yard, c.1925. Standing by the engine is his mate Tom Wilkins. (Museum)

A threshing machine, steam driven, 1920s and 30s. (Mrs B. Wallace)

Early 1900, Mr John Sale's men enjoy a much needed break, having their beaver (lunch). (Mrs B. Wallace)

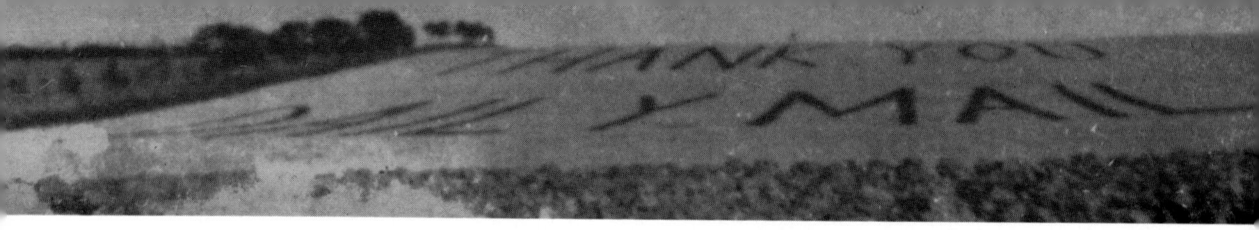

John Sale's tribute to the Daily Mail in 1929. Grown in mustard 39ft long letters, Mr Sale was expressing thanks for the Daily Mail's weather forecasts.
(O. Woodforde)

c. 1920. A steam ploughing engine in collision with its plough. The tangled heap was a double ended plough pulled from one side of a field to the other by two engines. Steam ploughing engines were owned by Gordon Cooper, Ashwell, William Hunt, Steeple Morden and Kendalls of Millow.
(Museum)

A much more tranquil scene from the 1920s.
(Mrs B. Wallace)

Haymakers, c.1880
These ladies refused to be "drawerer'd" until they had been home to change into clean aprons. They were photographed by Amy Critchley, Mrs Wolverley Fordham's sister in law.
(From a glass negative possessed by Richard Whitmore, TV personality)

1925 Forerunner of battery hens: but still allowed plenty of freedom.
(Mrs B. Wallace)

Noah Geeves in Farrows Farm yard, ready for the 1925 Bank Holiday Show.
(Mrs B. Wallace)

Two wonderful photos

Above: *Harvesting a Redlands Farm field off Station Road, c.1900. Harvesters proudly pose for the camera, with Sir George Fordham, shotgun on shoulder – truly a picture that tells a story.* (Mr & Mrs B. Northern)

Below: *The Holloway family, smallholders, harvesting in the early 1900s.* (Richard Whitmore)

The author's father on one of the first Fordson Tractors – early 1920s. (The author)

pargetry - oystershell, which was worked with a wooden comb, and honeycomb pattern, made with a small press consisting of a wooden base, containing several rows of steel hob nails, which when pressed into the soft plaster produced a honeycomb effect.

In the mid-1800s, when coprolite was being dug in the nearby fields, the house became a temporary pub known as the Tumble Down Dick. The farm buildings nearby consist of a mill built in 1908 (with red bricks made at Hitchin) to grind cattle foods and pump water for the horses, cattle and pigs. There was also a good range of stables, cattle pens, etc. built with local elm studwork covered with elm featheredge boarding, built about 1910. Alongside was a long, older building with thatched roof. Bluegates land extended more or less from the Bury park northwards towards Dunton.

In the 1920s **Ducklake Farm House** was divided into two dwellings. Part of it was occupied by Arthur Pickett, the farm bailiff, and his wife. It was a very ordinary, in fact shabby-looking house. It had dingy roughcast walls under a moss-covered plain tiled roof, and the small enclosed pebbled back yard was usually littered with straw. A low building which butted on to the back of the house was a dairy. On the street side was a long range of cart sheds open to the road, and at the end a little brick blacksmith's shop with a galvanised iron roof. Behind these buildings is a long tall timber framed and featheredge boarded barn. It also had a corrugated iron roof, but no doubt when it was built in the 17th century it was thatched with straw grown on the farm.

Arthur C Waldock, who was born about 1870 in the pindar's cottage, now owned by Mr G Coad, just over the river, remembered as a boy playing in the big barn and watching farmworkers flailing corn on the raised thrashing floor. He also watched Mr Snow Fordham trying his hand at the flail. The land belonging to Ducklake farm, apart from the adjoining meadow, stretched roughly northwards from the Morden road, with the Steeple Morden and Cambridgeshire boundary on one side and Northfield road on the other until it met the land of Kirby Manor.

Towards the end of the 1920s, the secretary's services came to an abrupt end. William H Wallace, the young member of an old Hertfordshire family, became farm manager and took up residence at Bluegates farm house. The farm bailiff retired about the same time, which left Ducklake house vacant. Mrs Fordham decided to have the house completely renovated. F.J. Bailey & Co., the Ashwell builders, stripped it out room by room. A huge open fireplace was discovered in the centre room - which was to become the entrance hall -two carved clunch fireplaces in the bedrooms and many beams. Whilst cutting a hole through one wall, where it was proposed to insert a window, 16th century frescoes representing mermaids, mermen and pomegranates, in red, green, brown and black were discovered, similar to the patterns of the damasks of Catherine of Aragon.

When repairing one of the bedroom ceilings, workmen found a small piece of alabaster sculpture which has been described as "the copulating couple". It naturally aroused great interest.

Behind the house, the untidy chicken houses and pig styes were cleared away leaving a view down to the river. Grass seed was sown, shrubs planted and fruit trees to form a very pleasant garden. The house was then let to Mrs Gladys Raikes, an old school friend of Mrs Fordham. A dividing strip led to a ford across the river, ending beside the thatched cottage which, until the enclosure award, was occupied by the pindar, the parish official who looked after the pound where the common holders' stray sheep or cattle were impounded. As the ford was no longer used and the right of way to it was overgrown, the parish council were only too pleased for Mrs Fordham to take it over. This also meant extending the existing cob wall to block off the entrance to the ford. So, round about 1930, the last section of genuine cob walling, complete with thatched capping, was built in Ashwell.

The original **Kirby Manor Farm House** is the gabled house in High Street, now a dentist's surgery. After the enclosure award, a new Kirby Manor FarmHouse was built on the North Field Road. The farmer was a Mr Brown, a bowler-hatted, bearded man. The land was owned by St John's College, Cambridge, and towards Ashwell met the Fordham land.

About **Mobbs Hole Farm**: most, if not all the land beyond Kirby Manor farm up to Whitegates and the boundaries of Bedfordshire and Cambridgeshire, had belonged to Ashwell parish. Over the centuries, generous persons had bequeathed "parcells" of land to Ashwell. The land was let annually to the highest bidder, and the annual income was given to buy a specified number of loaves of bread, hundredweights of coal or yards of flannel for poor persons. It had also to pay for apprenticing a certain number of village boys, all to be supervised by vestry officials.

Towards the end of the 19th century, after many bad harvests and poor corn prices, the tenant farmers either refused to or simply could not pay the rents, and there was no bread, coal, flannel or apprenticeships. Consequently, the church officials decided to sell the land and invest the money so that the charity could continue its good works, using the interest on those investments. Today the Ashwell charities are controlled by the Charity Commissioners and a local body of trustees, including the rector and churchwardens, who report annually to the parish meeting.

In the twenties this land was owned by Charles Murfitt and his son, Frank. The small farmhouse known as Mobbs Hole was a pub called the Labour in Vain during the coprolite period.

Some of the cottagers who were holders of common rights were allotted strips of land to compensate them for their loss. Usually these were soon sold off to the nearest farmer. William Pack, the blacksmith, had a few small fields, also Frank Christy who, in addition, rented from the parish a field known as Small Gains because the soil was poor. In the twenties, however, whilst picking brussels sprouts in this field, Bill Barton picked up a gold crown of James I. Along Ashwell Street, or the Ruddery as it was more commonly known, Samuel Evans, a carpenter and joiner who lived in and owned Alder Cottage, Lucas Lane, owned one field, and nearby, Henry Bonnett, the tailor, also owned a field, where his sons Jim and Douglas dug a well. The builder, J. W. Bailey, also owned land, including a meadow and an orchard along the Ruddery.

George Longley came to Ashwell just after the first world war and took over a field or two near the Fox public house on station road. George, a religious and very enterprising man, with a perpetual smile, was one of the forerunners of battery chicken farmers. He advertised in the "Christian Herald" for young Christian men to come to work and live in a sort of commune. The business flourished, sales of poultry and eggs increased and eventually a salesman was sent out over a wide area to sell, in addition to the usual chicken, pig, cat and dog food, a Longley special chicken feed called "Keep 'Em At It". A large van was used to deliver the orders out to the many customers. From

1932 until 1948, the publisher's father, Bert Gurney, Deacon at Zoar Strict Baptist Chapel, was the salesman.

At a later date Mr Longley set up a dairy at a time when Ashwell was well supplied with milk by Bluegates and the Co-op. To would-be customers a daily pint of milk was dropped on the doorstep without a message of any kind. At the end of the week the little roundsman knocked on the door to ask if he could make them regular customers. After a few years Sunnymead dairy closed.

Fruits of the Land

The advent of petrol-driven transport in the twenties brought about the decline of the horse population and with it the need for the hay crops of clover, sainfoin, lucerne and trefoil to feed the horses. These crops, after being cut, turned, dried and stacked by the farmer, were destined to feed thousands of transport horses in the towns and cities. John Inns of Stevenage was the chief hay buyer in this area, knew each farmer's acreage of hay, and at the appropriate time would make an offer. After some haggling the deal would be clinched. Then came the cutting, trussing and tying. For this, John Inns employed several expert hay tiers, two of whom lived at Hinxworth, Bob Rollins and Dan Fairy.

After removing the thatch from the haystack the tiers would attack it with a heavy, broad-bladed knife, about two feet six inches long and six inches wide. The hay was cut into sections roughly three feet by two feet, then placed in a huge hand-operated hay press, which reduced the depth of the truss to something like eighteen inches. Next, two lengths of binder twine were quickly passed round the truss and tied.

The next stage was the carting. Jack Carter, landlord of The Fox public house half way between Ashwell and the station, and Adam Page, who lived in a flint-faced cottage on the Kelshall road opposite the old tarmac runways of the Royal Flying Corps flight station, were the two local carters.

John Inns horses and carts were the smartest and best in the area, the carts always well painted dark blue outside, the shafts and inside the body a red-lead pink. A well-filled, leather-bound coconut fibre nose bag swung from the rear ladder. The well-groomed horses had ear protectors in summer to ward off the flies and always a selection of highly polished brasses with a small brass bell on top of the halter which tinkled as the horse's head moved methodically up and down on the hard pull to Ashwell station.

Here at the Great Northern sidings the trusses were loaded on to Inns' own trucks later to be coupled to a goods train and on to King's Cross. From now on the hay was called "green meat", at least that was how it was described by the London buyers. I remember, at a very early age, staying at Ilford with a great-uncle, Tom Bond, and his family. Thos. Bond and Sons were buyers of "green meat" by the truck load which they in turn sold to Selfridge's and other London stores, brewers and so on to feed the tremendous number of horses used to pull the provision vans, wagons and beer drays of those days.

Robert Christy, born at Westbury Farm, gave me the following note which is of particular interest in view of the enormous prices of both land and property in the 1980s. Also, in spite of the fact that John Inns could not write his name he became a millionaire, and had built both Baldock and Old Stevenage post offices, which he rented to the G.P.O. Look out for the large J.I. on the front of each of these post offices.

Robert Christy writes: "Before J.T. Mills came on the scene, my father told me that Westbury Farm, Farrows Farm and Bear Lane Farm were owned by a Mr Tinling. In October 1918, my father, and I understand Mr Sale too, was forced to buy his farm at a time of inflated prices caused by the war. My father's bid was topped by John Inns who bought the 290 acres and the farm house for £5,050, a considerable sum in those days. I remember Mr Inns coming to collect instalments of Dad's outstanding debt and making his mark; he couldn't write."

Small Holdings

Early this century, some radicals in agricultural areas discussed the possibility of providing small rented farms which could be worked by one or two men or a family. Sir Herbert Fordham of Odsey and his brother, Ernest Oswald Fordham of Odsey House, both Liberals (as all the Fordhams were), and directors of the family firm of brewers, were supporters of this idea. Their Tory opponents opposed it, and said of Sir Herbert, "Of course he will support it, provided it does not affect his land". The two Fordham brothers lived to see smallholdings set up; in fact, E.O. Fordham was appointed to the body which set up the Hertfordshire smallholdings.

At Ashwell, land towards Hinxworth, originally part of Squire Mills, the banker's estate, was divided into several holdings. Loves farm house was divided to form accommodation for two families, those of William Holloway and Cushi Harradine, with their holdings nearby. A further three Harradine brothers, Joshua, Arthur and Ezekiel, also had holdings. Stanley Jarman of Steeple Morden came to occupy the low-thatched cottage lower down the lane, with his land down towards The Cuckoo pub. Another holding further on known as Hinxworth Field Barns was farmed by Bert Bray, who kept some cows and delivered milk in Ashwell.

Allotments

Allotments were small plots that could be rented annually by cottagers who wished to supplement the vegetable crops grown on their cottage gardens. Here again the Fordham family were to the forefront. Fordham's, the brewers, owned the largest block of allotments. A large field adjoining their malting off Station Road was divided into scores of plots. Henry Bowman's map of Ashwell does not give the field a name, but I remember allotment holders called it "hangpost" or "hampost". Another allotment field just beyond the cemetery was called Baldwyns Corner, and a third in the area - called Paddocks. At the lower part of Lawyers Close, Gardiners Lane, was another allotment field, part of which was rented by Hertfordshire County Council for use by boys of Merchant Taylors' School.

Mr J.R. Page, the brewer, had a group of allotments on the Newnham road, where two bungalows have since been built. The Stag Benefit Society owned a small block next to its row of cottages in Lucas Lane, especially for members. The Ancient Order of Foresters very wisely bought a whole field towards the end of last century. It stretched from Back Street, where they built eight cottages for members, up to Ashwell Street, where they remain the last of Ashwell's original allotments still in use - a very valuable building site in the 1980s.

Fruit Growers

There were several fruit growers in Ashwell. James Bennett and his father before him had a large orchard in Bennetts Lane, where he grew both eating and cooking apples. Many of the old varieties, like "Jim", have now died out. There was a large, firm, red-striped apple called "beefin". Some of these could often be picked up in the spring, having survived in the grass during winter's frosts.

Next door to Jim in Bennetts Lane lived Tom Sansbury with his sister Kate, in the long narrow cottage, which had a thatched roof and whitewashed walls. Towards the end of the last century, however, it had been a public house called the New Found Out - a reference to the coprolites which were dug up in that area. Dan Smith was the landlord and sold beer brewed by Philips, the brewers in Royston. Apart from growing apples, Victoria plums, greengages, blackcurrants and narcissi, Tom Sansbury kept chickens and bees and was well known for his homemade wines.

The largest fruit grower of all was Mrs W.A. Fordham. Apart from a few fruit trees in the kitchen gardens in Gardiners Lane, there was an orchard in front of the Grange in the field known as 'Cock Shying Close'. My grandfather, James Lee, remembered a sort of fair being held there in the 1850s with stalls selling sweets and ginger-bread cockerels. But most of all, he remembered the kicking matches where strong men with heavy boots kicked each other until one fell and was unable to rise again. He could not tell me whether cock fights also took place there.

The other orchards were at Ashwell End house, Bluegates farm; Chapmans, adjoining the derelict cottage in Elbrook lane and the biggest and youngest of all where Bluegates Dairy now stands.

The Bury gardeners attended to the pruning, although there was a time when a young Oaklands-trained fruit expert came to look after the orchards. The gathering and storage of the fruit was in the hands of the two gardeners and the gardeners' boy. They were also responsible for the sale of the surplus fruit. Apples were stored at the old malting building behind the so-called Digswell Manor in High Street, where from autumn to spring on Saturday mornings one of the gardeners was on duty to sell to the village people for a few pence a peck or half peck measure, or to those who could afford it a bushel or half bushel.

There were several small dairies during the twenties. Bluegates farm kept a few cows, probably to supply milk, cream and butter for use at The Bury, with the surplus sold from a small shed at Redlands Grange. Here I remember Miss Alice Butt (later Mrs Rolly Worboys), a Land Army "girl", ladling out the milk with a metal pint or half-pint measure into whatever container the customer brought. That might be a jug, a tin plated or dark blue enamelled can with a lid and wire handle. A few cows were kept at Ducklake farm and the milk sold to people in that area.

Mr Thomas Wylie of Bear Lane farm kept several cows in the meadow behind the farm, now part of the council housing estate, and sold skimmed or unskimmed milk from the back door. At Dixies farm next door, Mr William Cooper kept several cows, which grazed either in Dixies meadow in front of the farm house or in Dixies Close which gave its name to the housing estate already mentioned. The cows were milked and the milk measured out to customers in the long tarred and feather-edge boarded barn alongside High Street.

There was one other dairyman in Ashwell. Bert Bray, who lived at West End and rented a Hertfordshire County Council smallholding at Hinxworth Field Barns had a small milk round and employed his cousin, John Dean, who delivered milk from a bicycle with a box sidecar.

Early in the twenties Mrs W.A. Fordham decided that Ashwell needed a modern dairy and daily deliveries. The old Bacon farm buildings in High Street were converted into a milking parlour and a new building was erected for cooling the milk, also to separate some of it for cream. The residue was used to feed the young calves which were raised at Ducklake farm.

Ashwell Pubs and their Landlords

Over the centuries Ashwell has had over thirty pubs. When I was at school, there were twelve; today there are four.

The Fox was a small flint-faced pub, the sign depicting a rather hungry fox. Adjacent to the Cinques cottages, it was a convenient halfway house for thirsty travellers between Ashwell station and the village. It was owned by E.K. & H. Fordham, the Ashwell brewers, and the landlord was John Carter who, true to his surname, was a carter employed by John Inns, the Stevenage hay merchant. It has been much altered, the flint face has been plastered and it is now a private house.

The Cricketers, alongside the recreation ground, had sold the beers of J.R. Page, the West End Ashwell brewer, but was taken over by Wells & Winch of Biggleswade about 1920. The landlord was David Potton, who also farmed a small amount of land. The Cricketers is now a private house.

The Wagon & Horses, at the junction of Lucas Lane with Springhead was, I believe, a Philips of Royston pub, when these brewers closed down in the twenties. Mr and Mrs Enever, the landlord and landlady, moved out and Mrs Kirchin moved in, complete with her shop and ice cream machines. It is also now a private house.

According to W. Branch Johnson's "Hertfordshire Inns", published in 1962, the early history of the **Three Tuns Hotel** is unclear. Before 1806 there were two small ale houses side by side - the Bay Tree, in existence in 1715 and the Three Tuns, established later. In 1806 Samuel Bowman, who occupied the Bay Tree in 1799, was licensed to the Three Tuns. At that time the hotel was surrounded by much more land than at present. The Pound and Lock up were on one side, the Statute Fair was held opposite.

Until the Board School was built in the 1870s the Three Tuns had the only large room in Ashwell. This was known as the Assembly room, where wedding parties, coroner's inquests and sales by auction could be held. I remember a Mr Roberts, an old soldier, being the landlord. A keen collector of old coins, he would send coins found by his customers to the British Museum for identification.

I believe the next landlord was Edwyn Bentley, who had been stationed at R.A.F. Henlow. He was a very popular landlord, was clerk to Ashwell Parish Council and rate collector for Ashwell Rural District Council. The Tuns was owned by Simpsons, the Baldock brewers, now Greene Kings.

The Stag was in High Street opposite Days the bakers. Mrs Covington was the landlady, and it was owned by Wrights, the Walkern brewers. When it closed, Letchworth Cooperative Society took it over as a grocery shop. When this closed in the 60s it was converted into two houses, one of which is named Stag House. A building behind the Stag was the headquarters of The Stag Club, a sick benefit society.

The gabled, timber-framed **Rose & Crown**, Branch Johnson thought was 16th century. In 1746 when it was first mentioned, it had a malting attached. It was owned by James Ind, a Baldock brewer in 1792, whose brother, Edmund, founded Ind Coopes, the Romford brewers. Simpsons of Baldock were the owners in the twenties and Francis Dilley, a retired naval man, was the landlord. It was the first Ashwell pub to install a wireless set. There was also a billiard room.

The Six Bells in Swan Street was part of that block of cottages at the entrance to the churchyard. The whole block was built around 1850, with the locally-made sun-dried clay, mud, fine chalk and chopped straw blocks known as clay bats, then rendered with a mixture of lime, sand and goat's hair. It was a Pages, later Wells and Winch beer house. Bowls were played in the back yard and Joseph Keeble was the landlord. Now it is part private house, and part incorporating Brenda Overton's Six Bells Gallery.

According to Branch Johnson there was in 1609 an **Angel** in Mill Street kept by James Wright and in 1633 a wine tavern kept by Valentine Lee called the **Wheatsheaf**. In 1854 the **Wheatsheaf** in Mill Lane was kept by Thos Worboys, but owned by E.K. & O. Fordham. In 1849 Fordhams foreclosed a mortgage on a house in Mill Street occupied by Worboys, together with an adjoining house recently built by him.

It could well be that the 1854 house became the **Bushel & Strike**, which is of about that period, and the older **Wheatsheaf** was pulled down. The Bushel was only a small beer house until about 1930. John Clark, the landlord, was also church clerk. The pub has been fully licensed for some years now and is owned by Charles Wells, the Bedford brewers. At the rear and adjoining it the old clubroom is now a restaurant. The clubroom was built during the latter half of the last century, when working men's sick benefit clubs came into being. The parish authorities (the rector, churchwardens and overseers of the poor) welcomed the clubs; in fact, the vestry minutes record the granting of certain sums of money to help found the clubs.

The Engine, a beer house in Back Street, was bought in 1836 by the landlord, John Bailey, an Ashwell builder, but in that same year Edward Fordham, a brewer of Odsey, took up a mortgage due to a debt for beer incurred by the landlord. When Bailey died in 1886 Edward King Fordham of Ashwell brewery foreclosed the mortgage. Some believe the pub was named after the steam threshing engine, others that it was without a name until steam railway engines passed through the parish in 1850. In the twenties the landlord was William F. Rand, a builder, who was followed by William Simon Beadle, a painter and decorator from Royston.

Opposite **The Cuckoo** Public House on the Hinxworth Road under a shady oak tree, just over the Ashwell boundary in a little hollow, was the coolest, clearest sparkling water, the Cuckoo spring. A little further back on that sharp bend of Hinxworth road was another of these springs of crystal clear water, known for years as Hungry well, where thirsty harvest workers -working up to thirteen hours a day - came to fill their bottles, after the cold milkless tea had run out.

Soon even these springs were to run dry. For a good many years, the Biggleswade

View from the Church Tower. (Town & Country News, 1932)
Front left to right: *The Bury Greenhouse, Mill Street Cottages.*
Centre: *Fordhams Brewery buildings, Maltings and the Brew er's house. In the distance the roofs and chimney stacks of Elbrook House. Note the masses of elm trees.*

Fordhams Maltings, built c.1900. (Town & Country News, 1932)
During World War I used as a German Prisoner of War Camp, and an Army Barracks during World War II; more recently R. White's Soft Drinks Stores. In 1990 converted into flats.

Fordham's bottling staff in the 1930s. (Town & Country News, 1932)

A 1900 photograph of staff of Page's Brewery, which ceased to exist in 1920. (Museum)

Above: *The Cricketers Inn, opposite the Recreation Ground, last drinks in the late 1940s.* (Museum)

Above left: *Delivering ales to the Six Bells pub in Swan Street, early 1900.* (T. Abbott)

Left: *The Three Tuns, pictured in 1876 during the Celebrations to mark the re-opening of the Merchant Taylors School.* (Museum)

Below left: *The Two Brewers in the High Street, c.1900.* (Robert Godsman)

Below: *The Wagon and Horses, Springhead, c.1910. Note the timber boarded cottages on the left, which originally housed Day's first bakery in Ashwell. Now demolished and the site of the Crabtree family home.* (Museum)

pumping station on the Great North Road had sufficient water to supply all its customers; in fact, about 1910, it was prepared to supply Ashwell as well, at a price. Then, when a few eccentric gentry installed bathrooms and actually bathed once a week, soon to be followed by more and more, the Biggleswade Water Board had to find an alternative supply. As pumping at the new Dunton works got into its stride, so not only did the Cuckoo and Hungry well springs dry up, the levels of the Quarry springs, the Westbury springs and our own Ashwell Springs went down, not to mention the complete disappearance of the old pond at Farrows farm.

Chalkmans Knoll, always referred to simply as **The Knoll**, was a Fordhams house. The landlord, Mr Collins was, I understand, blinded in the 1914-18 war, then trained as a mat maker at St Dunstan's. A sample of his work was in Ashwell church until fairly recently: a large doormat made of coconut fibre with "St Mary's Church" worked in black letters. There have been many theories as to the name of the pub. The most popular was that somewhere nearby there was at one time a tumulus. It is near the Iron Age fort of Arbury Banks and the Pancake Hill tumulus and part way between the ancient Ashwell Street and the Icknield Way.

The Knoll, built of clay bats, is probably mid-19th century. In its day the pub was a halfway house between Bygrave and Ashwell. It was the nearest pub to Bygrave, and it was a handy place for the men who worked in the nearby fields. It is now privately owned.

The Hare and Hounds at Slip End on the A505 about halfway between Baldock and Royston - another clay bat building of around 1850 - was a Philips of Royston pub. This section of the Icknield Way is Ashwell's boundary.

The pub is mentioned in the Hertfordshire County Sessions Rolls when the owner of an Ashwell windmill was mugged. It stood well back and if it was there today, with thousands travelling the road, I feel sure it would be a very popular pull-in. But when, during the years of depression, it closed, more people were walking from one workhouse casual ward to the next than there were cars. So it became neglected and eventually was pulled down.

John Law was landlord of **The Cuckoo** Public House, which stood on the boundaries of Ashwell and Hinxworth. The customers were mainly men working in the surrounding fields, people travelling from Ashwell to Hinxworth or Biggleswade, and on Sunday evenings, when it was the custom for families to go out for long walks and drop in at a pub for a glass of ale and mineral waters for the children. This was before motor traffic took away much of the pleasure of country walks.

Old Johnny Horner, as the landlord was nicknamed, had several sidelines to supplement the small income from the pub. He was an excellent shot: pheasants were rare in those days, but both types of partridge were quite common and there were plenty of rabbits and hares. He sold fruit from the orchard, and was a first class grower of standard roses.

Johnny knew exactly where every wild rose bush grew in the many hedges within a mile of the pub. He would collect hundreds of briars each year and when they were established in rows in his garden he would, at the correct season, insert a bud in each. Often he would prune and bud the wild rose bushes in the remote hedgerows of Nightshot, Bacceworth or Caldecote Bottom. I remember birdsnesting in that area and suddenly finding a large white rose, which my father said was a German rose named

Frau Carl something or other, and a little further on a beautiful pink moss rose. When the time was ripe Johnny would dig up the bushes to sell to his customers.

The publican's main and quite profitable sideline was in the shape of rows and rows of beehives. The Cuckoo was an ideal spot for the bee keeper. It was set in the midst of fields of red clover, pink sainfoin, blue flax - we called it linseed - and lucerne, yellow mustard and trefoil, not to mention the cornfields, scarlet with poppies or yellow with charlock, each producing a different flavoured and often a different textured honey.

The honey yield at The Cuckoo was so great in that extremely hot summer of 1921 that John Law took his honey by the ton cart load, in 28lb and 56lb metal containers, to Biggleswade station to be despatched to his many customers. John had gained his knowledge of bees not from books but from older beekeepers and by trial and error.

Sickness, Self Help and Societies

The sale of Ashwell's workhouse in 1836 and the formation of the Royston Union, with the building of Royston workhouse, which had accommodation for 300 paupers, hastened the introduction of a number of village benefit clubs. The Medical Club had been established in 1835. Members paid a weekly subscription and in return received free medical attention.

The Oddfellows, founded in the second half of the 19th Century, had one of the grander clubs, which within a few years boasted a membership of more than a hundred. The Ashwell Branch of The Ancient Order of Foresters was founded about the same time; a subscription of 5d. a week brought the member the generous sum of 12s. a week when ill.

The Foresters' headquarters was at the rear of the Bushel and Strike pub in Mill Street - in the building now used as a restaurant. I understand that this was one of the wealthiest clubs in the village. One night each month the members, some from surrounding villages, came to pay their subscriptions. In those days, long before television or radio, it was a place where, after working ten or twelve hours a day, old friends could meet for a chat, and if they so desired could continue the conversation over a beer in the pub. The club's officers received a small annual salary to compensate them for their work and regular attendance. They were usually employees of E.K. & H. Fordhams, the brewers. The members' subscriptions were invested in that company.

This club organised an annual feast day, when the officers wore bowler hats and blue serge suits with wide red or green sashes ornamented with large silver medallions. Some wore coloured aprons according to their status. They marched in procession round the village, two members proudly bearing the beautifully embroidered banner, preceded by the Ashwell Brass Band attired in their second-hand yeomanry uniforms. The procession returned to headquarters where members' wives had been busy roasting huge joints of meat and preparing the great feast - all to be washed down with Fordham's ales and Christy's minerals.

In 1892, the Foresters' club built several cottages in Back Street, to be rented by members. Behind the cottages, a block of allotments stretching up to Ashwell Street were for the use of members. Ancient timber-framed cottages in High Street were previously owned by the club as five cottages and let to the members.

With the introduction of the National Health Service the sons of members could not see the point of paying the club's subscriptions when they were already paying into a state scheme. Besides, they could now afford to buy motor cycles - a few even cars - to get about and see things and places their parents had only dreamed of. The cinema, for better or worse, was showing them an entirely different kind of life; so the club gradually faded away.

In 1959 the Foresters' club sold the old timber-framed cottages by auction. Much could be written about the sale and the purchase, anxious queries of councillors, the eviction order against the three tenants, partial demolition of the property, the visit of Anglia Television, the prompt action of the Hertfordshire Society, a temporary preservation order by the then Minister of Housing, issued within two days and, later, compulsory purchase by the County Council. Finally came restoration and eventual sale to private buyers. Maybe one day the story will be told in full.

Lastly, the Back Street cottages were sold to the sitting tenants and all that remained was for the club to be wound up. The Foresters' banner was lost between the wars. I have a photograph when it headed a procession at the end of the Great War, and fortunately some of the sashes and other regalia were given to Ashwell Museum.

The Bushel and Strike clubroom was used for a number of purposes. For some years the Royal Antedeluvian Order of Buffaloes, or "Buffs", met here, then with the founding of the Royal British Legion after the First World War this also became their meeting place.

When John Clark was the landlord and church clerk, the Rev. S.W.P. Webb held the winter Sunday school "treats" in the clubroom. The scrubbed deal tables were laden with paste and jam sandwiches, slices of currant and seed cakes, and mugs of weak tea. The summer treats were held in the Bury meadow where there were cricket and rounders, three-legged and other races, and of course a feast of sandwiches and cakes, with mineral waters kindly donated by Messrs A. & C. Christy.

The treat always ended with a mad scramble for the pear drops which fell in the grass after the rector had tossed them up in the air. He was a pear drop fanatic. Even at singing practice on Thursday after school and full choir practice on Friday evenings he passed round the pear drops. Perhaps the rector had shares in Garratt & Cannon, the Hitchin confectioners!

There was at one time an Ashwell club known as the Thursday Club. The only trace is a painted wooden box in Ashwell Museum. The box has three locks. Apparently it contained the club's books and records and could only be opened by three officials, each with his own key. It contained the chairman's gavel and the death certificate of a member who, I believe, was drowned in the river Thames.

I do know a little about the Stag Sick Benefit Club because I became a member when, at the age of 14, I started work. The monthly meetings were held in the clubroom, a small brick building with a corrugated iron roof in the garden behind the Stag Public House. It was approached by a gate in Swan Street. This club owned cottages in Lucas Lane with allotments adjoining. Other cottages were near the Springs and in Silver Street, all let to club members.

At the annual general meeting, the officers and members made any necessary amendments to the rather strict rules. There were no frills, neither sashes nor feasts. You paid your dues and if you were sick you received a certificate from the doctor and in due course a club official brought you the stipulated amount. Some of the officers were employed at Fordhams brewery. This club suffered the same fate as the Foresters, when the young men refused to join. So after a general meeting it was decided to sell the cottages and allotments, but unlike the Foresters the assets were shared among the members.

Ashwell Accidental Aid Society, open to anyone who cared to pay the small quarterly subscription, was very popular with working men, especially building workers, who were more prone to accidents than most. Meetings were held for some years in the Technical Room (now Parish Room). Again, with falling membership, the club folded in 1968 dividing its assets among the members.

Some public houses organised slate clubs for their customers. There was a Clothing club and a Coal club, where the members saved regularly throughout the year to buy clothes and coal. Most cottagers kept one or more pigs in the sty at the bottom of the garden and for a few pence a week could insure against the loss of a pig. At a vestry meeting in 1854, Mr Sale successfully proposed that a twopenny rate be levied to help the labourers' benefit clubs.

Ashwell & District Nursing Association was founded in 1897 to commemorate the Diamond Jubilee of Queen Victoria, and continued into the 1940s. The association was run by a committee, and the funds to support a full time nurse came from subscriptions. Nurse Moss was, I believe, the first parish nurse, succeeded in 1917 by Nurse Reading. The third was Nurse Gwenda Westrope, formerly Williams.

Nurse was responsible for school visits when she weighed and measured the children and, of course, checked their heads for lice. She also worked in conjunction with Dr R.E.H. Woodforde throughout his large area in all cases of illness, except midwifery of which he was not very fond, though ready to act if complications set in.

King Dick, Builder

It was not until about the last quarter of the nineteenth century that builders as such came into being in Ashwell. Families like the Carpenter and Undertaker brothers Walter, Samuel and Herbert Picking and Master Bricklayers, Thorne and Bailey, each employing a few men, competed for the work. Thorne had the contract to build the Merchant Taylors' School extension in 1876, but Frederick Bailey got the contract to build the Board school for £2,000 and from then on he did most of the building work in and around Ashwell.

"King Dick", as he was nicknamed by his men, flourished, bought land and soon became quite a village elder, and as his son John took over the business, he was able to retire with his wife to the house at the top of Bear Lane, which is now a factory. John Bailey married Hilda Flitton of Flitton's Mill, Station Road, Steeple Morden. They lived with their daughter Peggy in the Red House at the entrance to the builders' yard in Silver Street.

When in 1925, at the age of 14, I began work, F.J. Bailey & Co was regarded as one of the best building firms in the area. About fifty men were employed with Walter Bray the manager, Fred Bray and Tom Barnes as general foremen, plus joiners, carpenters, bricklayers, painters, timber men, sawyers, a lorry driver, labourers and carters.

Apart from Ashwell employees, they cycled in from Royston, Barley, Bassingbourn, Litlington, Steeple Morden and Hinxworth. Work commenced at 7 a.m., breakfast was 8.30-9, midday break 1-2 p.m., then on to 5.30 p.m. and Saturday 7 a.m.-12. Outside a small office on Friday, pay day, the men queued up at 5.30 p.m., foremen first, followed by tradesmen, labourers and apprentice boys last. There was cement in two hundredweight jute sacks from the Arlesey cement works, nails in 56lb jute sacks; paint in basic colours in gallon cans; distemper, green, cream or white in one hundredweight drums, ceilingite (a smelly white stuff used to whiten ceilings) in half hundredweight wooden kegs; tanks of pure turpentine and linseed oil, drums of linseed putty and crates of glass. Paints were mixed by hand to customers' orders. On one wall the paint was almost an inch thick, where over the years painters had tried out their mixtures.

In the large joiners' shop were panel doors, framed, ledged and braced doors, door frames and linings, window sashes and frames; all the timber articles which today are mass produced, were made by hand. Up the steep hill above the carpenters' shop was the English timber yard. Mr Bailey bought standing timber, oak, elm, beech, ash and fir and employed two or three men equipped with cross-cut and hand saws to cut down and bring home the tree trunks by means of a Burrell traction engine and timber carriage. Here it was stacked until it was ready to be taken into the sawmill to be cut into coffin boards, gate or fence posts, pales or rails, door or window sills.

The sawmill was a draughty, bodged up building housing two machine saws and a planing machine, all powered by a very crude gas engine, which seemed to be fuelled by bark from the sawn up timber.

I understand this sawmill was set up just before or in the early days of the first World War, when the firm had a government contract for ammunition boxes and bobbins which were used as minesweeper net floats. In the twenties, the sawmill was in the hands of Bill Picking (a descendant of the old firm of Sam, Walt and Herb Picking) and Albert Hall, both old soldiers. For nine old pence, employees could fill a barrow with offcuts which would keep a home fire burning for several days.

Lime burning was another of Mr Bailey's enterprises. At the top of Bear Lane, where two bungalows have since been built, there was a chalk quarry, with at one time two lime kilns. Peter Skerman, a well-built bearded man, was the lime burner. The kiln was a funnel-shaped structure ten or twelve feet deep lined with fire bricks. To reach the base it was necessary to negotiate several crude steps, where a slatted gate led to an underground sort of cave. Here a small fire was laid inside the furnace. Then, from above, Peter shovelled in alternate layers of chalk and fine coal until the funnel was filled to ground level. In due course the whole mass was slowly burning issuing a greyish white smoke, which had a ghostly sort of smell. When the lime was burned to Peter's satisfaction, he would withdraw the large three-pronged fork at the base of the furnace which released the lumps of hot lime into the cave, and so the process would be repeated.

Colour-washing of the exterior of buildings required a very special mix. Lump lime was placed in a large tub or tank, boiling water added and the tank covered until the lumps were dissolved in the hot smooth paste. Then pure linseed oil, Russian tallow and copperas (green iron sulphate crystals) were added and stirred in with more water. After 24 hours this could be diluted ready for application. If the building was to be coloured pink, red ochre powder was stirred in until the correct shade was produced, but the favourite Ashwell colour was a creamy yellow, made by carefully mixing in yellow ochre and brown umber powder.

At one end of the lime kiln field some old buildings, which had probably been cattle sheds, were used to store new timber, salvaged window and door frames, staircases, etc. The rest of the field was covered with stacks of bricks of every type, new glazed drainpipes and fittings, clay agricultural pipes from the Arlesey kilns, chimneypots new and old, stone slabs and slate slabs, roofing slates and tiles, pantiles, ridge tiles, hip tiles, valley tiles, quarry tiles, many of which were leftovers from buildings ever since Baileys built the Board school in 1878.

In the twenties and thirties, when a builder received the contract to build, he employed men to dig the trenches for the foundations, to mix the concrete by hand for the foundations, lay the bricks, cut and fix the floor joists and floors, fix the tiles, plaster the ceilings and walls, make and fix all the woodwork, the drains, the water supply, even dig the well if necessary. In fact, he saw it through from start to finish.

Work undertaken by Baileys varied from new building to alterations and restoration to old houses, pubs and churches, the Fordham estates at Ashwell and Odsey and the Peel estate at Eyeworth, Hertfordshire County Council small holdings and many more. Mr Bailey had some architectural skills. He became surveyor to Fordhams, the Ashwell brewers, and Simpsons, the Baldock brewers, which brought much work for the firm in alterations and extensions to The Coach & Horses, The Marquis of Lorne and The Yorkshire Grey at Stevenage, The Railway Hotel at Knebworth, The Wellington at Welwyn, the Red Hart at Hitchin, the re-building of the Rose & Crown at Hoddesdon and many more.

In 1921 the firm built some of the first council houses, at Bygrave, Newnham and Radwell, and in 1926, twenty-six at Station Road, Ashwell in 52 weeks.

John Bailey was, in his early days, a keen cricketer. In 1920 the Baileys moved into Westbury House, which they greatly improved, and developed the gardens. Without a son to carry on the business, he retired in 1934.

However, it was not the end of the building firm. The Manager, Walter A. Bray, with his brother Fred, the general foreman, took over, together with most of the work force and founded W. A. & F. Bray Builders, eventually settling in the West End premises where younger Brays still carry on the business.

William Frederick Rand, a carpenter and joiner, who had been employed by Baileys at the end of the First World War, set up in business as a Builder and Undertaker. At that time he was landlord of The Engine Public House in Back Street. At first he used the pub's yard and premises for his business, but after a time he acquired Woodlands in High Street where there were much larger premises. He had an agreement with Benjamin Christy of Westbury farm whereby in exchange for the use of the lime kiln at the Hinxworth road chalk quarries, he would undertake all essential building repairs to Westbury farmhouse and buildings. W.F. Rand sold part of his garden with the tennis court and built the house called Wellesbourne on it for Charles Walker, the Baldock and District Excise Officer. The firm died out in the early 1940s.

Ashwell Museum: Origins and achievements

It was back in 1921 that Neville Christy, Jack Christy and I made the first attempt to form a museum, encouraged by Morgan Biles, headmaster of the Ashwell Merchant Taylors' School, E.F.D. Bloom, HM Inspector of Schools, and T.W. Latchmore, who cycled over from Hitchin to take school photographs.

The first museum was housed in a lean-to greenhouse at Kirby Manor, and the exhibits were an odd assortment, a grass snake preserved in a pickle jar, two boxes of dried South African flowers, some fossils, local birds' eggs, a rabbit skull and a few Roman and British coins.

Frank Dilley, whose father was landlord of the Rose and Crown, joined us with an offering of two Boer war shells, and an Austrian soldier's helmet, then John Bray followed with a piece of coral and some ammonite fossils. The collection did not grow and, after a few years, we divided the spoils.

It was not until 1927 that John Bray and I decided to make a fresh start. John's parents allowed us the use of a garden shed at Red House in Silver Street. We formed a rambling club, and searched the chalk quarries and sand pits for fossils; Ashwell people turned out their unwanted bits and pieces until we filled the shed with a reasonable collection. We used to hand over the contents of the visitors' box to the Ashwell Church Tower Restoration Fund.

In July, 1928, we were invited to give a museum exhibition at a church garden party. It was well attended and a number of people expressed their surprise at the size and quality of our collection. As a result of this exhibition a Museum Committee was formed to purchase a suitable cottage.

Early in the sixteenth century Ashwell was a flourishing market town; the principal manor was owned by the Abbot of Westminster who, it is believed, ordered an office to be built on the market square, facing down Mill Street towards the church. The office, built with stout oak timbers, infilled with wattle and daub and a thatched roof, was for the use of the Abbot's steward to keep records of the tithes of the 4,000 acres of Ashwell land.

Here also the market traders would come to pay their dues. In the early nineteenth century this was known as the Town House. In 1841, it was modernised, the thatch was replaced with pantiles, small windows inserted, and the timbers encased in plaster. For a time it was occupied by Sarah Ripsher, who ran a straw plaiting school, then it became a tailor's shop, and finally a cottage until, in the mid 1920s, it was condemned by the housing authority.

This building, our committee decided, was to become Ashwell Village Museum. Ernest Fordham, our chairman, persuaded John Bray and me, both teenagers, to negotiate with the owner, Mark Crump, the well-known Ashwell butcher. We explained that our hobby had outgrown its present home, and that with voluntary labour we hoped to repair the cottage and tidy up the corner of Alms Lane and Swan Street. So for the sum of £25 the freehold came into our hands, and with it the task of rebuilding the chimney jambs, taking out the windows and the complete stripping of lath and plaster to reveal the timber frame as it was until 1841.

A local appeal brought in about £40. At this stage Sir William Gentle, Kt. was

The condemned cottage bought for £25 in 1929 to become Ashwell Village Museum in 1930. (Museum)

Peter Skerman. Lime burner for F.J. Bailey & Co. for many years. In 1930 he became Caretaker of Ashwell Museum. (Museum)

Restored to its original condition when it was built as the Abbot of Westminster's Tithe Office.
Left to right: *Peter Skerman, John Bray & Albert Sheldrick.*

Albert Sheldrick and John Bray at Ashwell Museum. Their collection started in 1927 and moved into the old Town House, originall y the Tithe Office of the Abbot of Westminster, in November 1930.
(Photograph by Sunday Pictorial, 1932.)

Below:
Part of the interior display.
(Royal Commission on Historical Monuments, 1930s)

invited to subscribe. He was born in Ashwell and later became Chief Constable of Brighton. Sir William offered not only to employ William Weir, of the Society for the Protection of Ancient Buildings, and pay for the complete restoration of the cottage by Messrs. F.J. Bailey & Co., the Ashwell builders, but to set up a trust to administer the museum with the six committee members as trustees.

So while Hitchin Regional Surveyors, and the Royston Crows were dreaming of museums for their respective towns, Ashwell Village Museum was officially opened by Sir William before a large gathering on Saturday 29th November, 1930.

A body of annual subscribers known as the Friends of Ashwell Museum, together with the proceeds of the visitors' box, covered the expenses such as rates, insurance, light, heat and repairs. Peter Skerman, a retired lime burner, who lived nearby was appointed custodian. A visitor could knock on Peter's door at any time and be admitted to the museum, unless he was imbibing at the Rose and Crown. Peter received ninepence per week, which in those days bought one ounce of tobacco and one box of matches, or two pints of mild and a box of matches. He also had the use of the museum garden, where he grew vegetables.

A report on Ashwell Museum by the Carnegie Trust in 1958 stated: "Finance, subscriptions and donations £20 a year, a further sum of £5 annually by the Herts County Council as a grant for educational services rendered. With this tiny income a museum service has been maintained and the building kept in repair. There is no professional staff, all the work here has been done as a labour of love by the curator and his fellow trustees. The collections, purely local, include natural science, archaeology and folk life. The material is of good quality and it is well labelled and well cared for. This report should not end without a tribute to the work which has been done by this museum, and the influence which it must have had on the lives and understanding of the people in this area".

The opening of the museum to visitors on Sundays from 3 p.m. to 5.30 p.m., and at other times by appointment, is in the hands of the Friends of Ashwell Village Museum.

Postscript

From 1939-1945 we were involved in Hitler's War and the War in the Far East. Anthony Hill, George Page, Willy Pettengell, and Doug Waldock were among those who did not come back.

The Rev Henry Martindale, Rector from 1941-1946, was followed by the Rev John F. B. Keith, 1946-1951, an ex-serviceman and probably Ashwell's youngest parson this century. The Keiths emigrated to New Zealand. Another short stay Rector was the Rev Geoffrey Oakshott, 1951-1953, to be followed by the Rev John J Catterick (later Canon Catterick) 1953-1977. Jack Catterick was very popular and with his four chorister sons founded the well known Ashwell Festival. In July 1969 the Queen Mother paid a private visit to Ashwell Museum. Dr Fergus Moynihan took over the practice on the retirement of his father in 1973 and in 1976 the Wardens of the Worshipful Company of Merchant Taylors came to Ashwell in style to celebrate the 100th Anniversary of the re-opening of their school.

The 60s had brought pop music, divorce, common law wives and one parent families. From the United Stated we had imported supermarkets, credit cards and drugs and as we moved into the 70s and 80s we saw pop stars living in mansions, football, our national sport, marred by hooligans, became big business, with players bought and sold for millions of pounds.

Living in renovated barns, once the home of horses, cows and pigs, has become the 'in thing'. People speak with 'hindsight' and 'at the end of the day' although we still do not know which day, and reiterate with boring repetitiveness "see what I mean" etc. We old folk used to say 'It's up to you', the smart people have changed it to 'It's down to you'.

In 1983 Flo Worboys retired after a record 60 years as Ashwell's post lady. She was awarded the B.E.M. for her services in the New Year's Honours List in 1982.

In the 80s came spiralling house prices: workmen's cottages built for £80 a pair in 1890 sold for £60,000 to £80,000 each. Dixies Cottage, rented by my parents for 2s 6d per week and bought by them in 1920 for £100, was recently sold for around £250,000.

During these years of multiple change the Rev John Mullett was Rector (1977-1990) warmly remembered by his many friends, those he visited in hospital, the sick and bereaved. His ministry was also notable for substantial fundraising for church renovation projects.

I have met the present Rector, the Rev Patrick Bright. Himself an artist, he will appreciate the paintings of Ashwell by Charlotte Morice, daughter of the Rev Henry Morice, 1812-1850, which were bequeathed to Ashwell Rectory by one of her descendants.

From time to time my wife and I return to Ashwell to visit relations and friends. We look down on the village from Claybush or Newnham Hill, wander along the Caldecote Bridleway or the little lane newly named after diminutive Rolly Worboys, who delivered Westrope's paraffin oil with his little truck.

Looking over the fence, the Bury has not changed since Sir Edwyn Lutyens altered the front elevation in the early 1920s. I can still see Mrs Fordham cutting roses or digging out plaintains with her spud. What would she think of the 1990s? I doubt whether her fourpence would even purchase the pepper and salt for a dinner today.

What would she see if she cycled round Ashwell today? Leaving the Bury she would find the Brewery replaced by Fordham Close, with a few houses facing the little River Rhee. Her eyebrows would be raised at the Mill House, but the recently installed water wheel and the Maltings conversion would please, as would the knowledge that the August Bank Holiday Show at Elbrook meadow is still a great success. There would be sadness at the loss of the elm trees through Dutch Elm disease, interest in the re-siting of Reg Fitzgerald's newly-built garage moving from its unsuitable locality in Swan Street, she would compliment the Parish Council on the excellent condition of the Cemetery, the Recreation Ground, the Children's Play Area and, of course, Ashwell Springs, in spite of recent dry summers.

She could call at the Three Tuns for coffee, as the hotel is now open all day and boasts a good lunch and dinner menu, plus accommodation. Her attention would be drawn to Jessamine House, where the Great Fire ended in 1850, now the Headquarters of the Veteran Car Club of Great Britain. Could it be that Doctor Woodforde's de Dion

Bouton, Ashwell's first car, is owned by one of its members?

Many a village has lost its Post Office; but Ashwell's still remains, selling an assortment of Greetings Cards, Stationery, Confectionery and packets of crisps for Ashwell's hungry children returning from schools at Royston, Baldock, Letchworth and Hitchin. Secondary school education in Ashwell ended in 1947. Next door to the Post Office, Barclays Bank's staff of two will attend to their customers until 1.30 pm, when they will duly return to the parent branch at Royston. The corner shop formerly run by Mrs Searle, who died recently, has long been part of a dwelling house.

Carefully crossing the road, as traffic is a hazard to a degree quite unknown before 1939, Mrs Fordham would sadly note the disappearance of Silas Worboys' Wheelwright Shop, and further down the High Street miss the aroma of freshly ground coffee, bacon and other goodies. Westrope's shop as such is no more. It is now two units - one a Greengrocer, the other a Pharmacy run by a charming and knowledgeable Indian lady. Russells, formerly J. R. Burton's Chemist's shop, is now just a window through which to see revolving displays of houses for sale. The Butcher's shop, where Eddie Brown smoked his cigarettes down to the last fraction of an inch, is now part of Ventnor House and the slaughterhouse now a children's playroom. On the other side of the road Dilley's Greengrocers, Winnie Stamford's Wool shop and the Bicycle Shop of Bert Collis, another inveterate smoker, have all gone. Henry Bonnett and sons, Jim and Douglas, the tailors, are also no more. Across Church Lane Fanny Adkins' 'Window to Watch' is now a private residence, but until 1990 was the Surgery. Doctors John and Sheila Moynihan, who retired some years ago, must envy their son, Doctor Fergus Moynihan and his partners at the new purpose-built Health Centre in Lawyer's Close, a far cry from the Mount, where there was room only for three patients in the waiting room.

New houses have replaced Turner's (earlier Ketteridge's) garage. The Co-op Shop, originally the Stag public house, has been converted into two houses.

In spite of intense competition from the Supermarkets, one Baker remains. Days of Ashwell, with shops at Royston and Baldock and an outlet at Letchworth. In 1989, Days won the prestigious Baker of the Year competition, organised by BBC Television's programme - Food and Drink.

The Butcher's shop of Tommy Dennis is no more, the brightly ornamented front has been removed, the bull's head with flashing eyes now adorns Chapmans, the Baldock Butcher's shop, and has now been amalgamated with J. H. Christy's, the Grocers, now known as the Village Stores, run by a hard-working Punjabi family, open all hours (or most of them). A Dentist now occupies the Newsagent' Shop, once belonging to A. & C. Christy. The Telephone Exchange has replaced the Mineral Water Factory and a private swimming pool sunk in the coalyard. The tiny Shoe Repair shop of Les Worboys has disappeared, leaving a car park and pleasant garden to attract customers to eat or drink at the Rose & Crown in the heart of Ashwell. Across the road, the Blacksmith's forge of William and Jim Bean has also gone. The Court House of the Manor of Westbury Nurnuyts (still wrongly named Digswell Manor) has had much renovation.

Mrs Fordham would miss the smell of cows and the clatter of milk churns from her 1920's dairy, now named Bacons Yard, with its attractive houses and pocket handkerchief-sized gardens. Ashwell now has two hairdressers, one in the High Street, the other in

Dixies old farmyard. Neighing horses, squealing pigs, wandering chickens and mooing cows have been replaced by business enterprises, publicity consultants, a florist, a beauty salon, and expensively renovated barns house newcomers to Ashwell.

The 18th Century Dove House can still be seen behind the farmhouse garden, but Dixies orchard, sadly known as "Dockland", is now overgrown with nettles and dock leaves smothering the circle of rare ornithalagum utans. Wilsons Lane is named after a Cavalier soldier, Robert Wilson, who was reported to the Magistrates in 1646 for having said, 'When the Roundheads come to Ashwell I will show them the houses of the Roundheads and where to plunder'. William Goodchild, known in the neighbourhood as Billy Roundarse, lived here in the 1920s. Mrs Fordham would remember him, but especially Billy's daughter, Maud. When she came to object to the replacement of small leaded windows by larger paned sashes, Maud told her to mind her own business and added "Would you like little windows in the Bury?". Little has changed at West End. She could see some housing development at Westbury Farm, where John Berridge preached to the 18th Century Dissenters. Making a quick visit to the Village Hall, she would be pleased to see its recent improvements and the continued use of the Scout Hut. In Back Street Jack 'Turkey' Worboys' shop has gone, houses built where Leopold Day's chickens ran free. The Dixies Farm cart hovel and the iron pump have been replaced by houses. Where Bear Farm's buildings stood, houses have been built by the Ashwell Housing Association.

Although the Head Teacher's house has been pulled down, the Board School flourishes in Silver Street, much extended and improved, and attended by over 120 pupils. Bailey's, the Builder's carpenter's shop, is now used for furniture stripping and repair, and the timberyard now a vehicle repair business. Angell's Meadow is now filled with houses. One Butcher has survived, Crumps in Mill Street, run by Mark Crump's grandsons, a magnet for customers from far and wide and, with Days, the last of the 1920's family and retailing businesses.

In Mill Street, Seven Springs Gallery displays the art and craft of Pauline and Marie Whitby. The Six Bells Gallery (formerly the Six Bells pub) in Swan Street, run by Brenda Overton, indicates the interest in her paintings, sketches and objet d'art.

Ashwell's industry, before 1939, centred around Farming and Brewing. The latter has gone and as we approach the year 2000, farming remains a prime industry, but new methods have radically cut its labour force. Farmer, Frank Brown, said to my publisher in 1940, "The internal combustion engine has ruined farming". It has certainly made a tremendous difference. Ashwell's biggest single employer is now Days the Bakers, with a staff of over 40. Cooke Engineering, with 30 employees making nuts and bolts etc, is in the building where Henry Leverett launched his 'Olde Tin Can' and Ashwell's first bus service. Small units connected with the Computer Industry inhabit part of Dixies, while at West End, I.D. Products make wooden fitments for the Building Industry. Close by, William Bray carries on the building business. Beacon Developments on Beaconleg Hill, Station Road, design and develop engineering equipment.

The High Street Dairy in 1969 moved nearer to Bluegates Farm but George Longley's Dairy and Poultry Foods business has long been replaced by Sunnymead Orchard, an estate of mobile (or rather, immobile) homes. What a busy day Mrs Fordham would have had, jumping on and off her bicycle as she toured the village. I can just imagine her nods of approval at the restored Forresters Cottages and the many well kept properties.

She would be pleased to find the Gardiners Lane cob wall well preserved, but regret the loss of her kitchen garden which was behind the wall. Some doubt as to the design, albeit not the provision, of Wolverley House, the Museum extension and a number of the post war buildings; this, she would be told, is progress.

After a quick check on the new Rector and a visit to the Church, she would smile at the new sign "Rollys Lane" and express her pleasure at the sight of horses at the Bury stables and the restored Mill Street cottages, and the Bury, in far better condition than when she departed. Congratulations are due to her great-nephew, Michael Gurney Sheppard, on his stewardship of the estate's farms, houses and cottages and to Mrs Sheppard for care of the gardens, especially the yew hedges and the mulberry tree.

If Mrs Fordham had had access to the document discovered by Mrs Wallace to which I refer at the beginning of this book, she would have pondered on the changes which have affected every part of village life. Looking at the list of occupations she would know that we no longer have horse slaughterers, speechmakers, malsters, quack doctors, tailors, drapers, brewers, shoemakers, yeast retailers, millers, blacksmiths, excisemen, clock repairers, wheelwrights or church clock winders. But we can boast of Butcher, Baker, Candlestick maker, Photographer, Furniture makers and Restorers, a Beauty Therapist, Child minders, Designers, Graphic and otherwise, a whole range of Consultants, a Tree Surgeon, a Reflexologist, Pottery makers, a Wood Turner, a Thimble case maker, Word Processor Operators, Electricians, Log Suppliers, Newsagents and many more.

We still have a visiting Chimney Sweep and coal is supplied by a merchant from outside Ashwell and, similarly, oil for central heating. British Gas invaded Ashwell in June 1991 to make gas available to its inhabitants, most of whom did not want it. I remember when, in the early 1930s, Ashwell folk asked for gas to be laid on from Baldock, their request was turned down. A number of clubs, societies and organisations prove the village still retains its community spirit, while its surviving churches, Church of England, Baptist and United Reformed, are well supported. We have already mentioned two of Ashwell's four remaining hostelries. The other two, the Bushel & Strike in Mill Street is renowned for its food, and the Engine in Back Street is now transforming its sawdust image to a more contemporary guise. All this points to a picture of a very busy Ashwell but, if it is tranquillity you wish for, there are plenty of highways and byways close at hand.

Mrs Fordham's favourite walk, and mine, was along Buttway where Tony Oyston grows king cups in the stream and further on willow herb, brooklime and waterbitney still grow. My Aunt Hilda used the leaves of the Waterbitney to make a soothing ointment, but that was over seventy years ago - or to put it another way - in the very different world of Ashwell before 1939.

List of Subscribers

MARY ANDERSON, 9 KINGSLAND TERRACE, ASHWELL, HERTS. 2.3.1930

OLIVE & JOHN ANDERSON, 23 KINGSLAND WAY, ASHWELL, HERTS.

MR. & MRS. R. J. ANNETTS, 29 RIDGEWAY ROAD, SALISBURY, WILTS.

GEORGE BARTON, 73 WOLVERLEY HOUSE, GARDINERS LANE, ASHWELL, HERTS.

DAVID & MARY BILLSON, ELM TREE COTTAGE, LETCHWORTH LANE, LETCHWORTH, HERTS.

CLIFF AND JOHN BONNETT, 79 STATION ROAD, ASHWELL, HERTS.

THE REV. & MRS. PATRICK BRIGHT, THE RECTORY, ASHWELL, HERTS.

PAULINE AND PETER BROOK, WARREN LODGE, 91 BACK STREET, ASHWELL, HERTS.

EVELYN C. BROWN, 20 HODWELL, ASHWELL, HERTS.

SHEILA AND PETER BRYANT, 64 ASHWELL STREET, ASHWELL, HERTS.

HARRY AND AUDREY BULLARD, 81 BACK STREET, ASHWELL, HERTS.

EMMA BULLARD, 31 BACK STREET, ASHWELL, HERTS.

BRIAN & VAL BUSBY, 4 WOODFORDE CLOSE, ASHWELL, HERTS.

MARGARET, JOHN, MIKE AND JANE BUSHELL, RISS HOUSE, SHAROW, RIPON, NORTH YORKS.

CHRISTOPHER AND CAROL CATTERICK, 9 FOURACRE, FENSTANTON, CAMBS.

JUDITH E. CATTERICK, BECKETS, 20 HODWELL, ASHWELL, HERTS.

ANTHONY AND ANITA CATTERICK, 59 THE CRESCENT, ABBOTS LANGLEY, HERTS.

MICHAEL AND EVELYN CATTERICK, 26 FAIRFIELD ROAD, ALDEBURGH, SUFFOLK.

ALEC & JANET CHENNELLS, BELLBINE COTTAGE, ASHWELL, HERTS.

MR. AND MRS. K. COILEY, 8 LUCAS LANE, ASHWELL, HERTS.

GRAHAM AND SUSAN COLLINS, 8 NURSERY CLOSE, BIGGLESWADE, BEDS.

LINDSAY AND ANNE COLQUHOUN, BEAR HOUSE, ASHWELL, HERTS.

IAIN COLQUHOUN, BEAR HOUSE, ASHWELL, HERTS.

ALISON M. C. COLQUHOUN, BEAR HOUSE, ASHWELL, HERTS.

ANDREW AND PAM COLQUHOUN, THE BEECHES, WENDOVER, BUCKS.

LACHLAN N. COLQUHOUN, BEAR HOUSE, ASHWELL, HERTS.

MAY AND GEOFF COOK, "ASHBROOK", 10 LUCAS LANE, ASHWELL, HERTS.

MAVIS & JAMES CRABTREE, RHEE HOUSE, SPRINGHEAD, ASHWELL, HERTS.

PHILIP AND GERALDINE CRUMP, 15 SWAN STREET, ASHWELL, HERTS.

ALISON DALBY AND STUART CUNNINGHAM, OWL COTTAGE, CHURCH PATH, ASHWELL, HERTS.

WILLIAM J. DAVIES, 3 FOX HILL, GUILDEN MORDEN, CAMBS.

MR. S. DILLEY, FORMERLY OF SPRINGS COTTAGE, HIGH STREET, ASHWELL, HERTS.

MRS. ETHEL M. DILLEY, 39 WOLVERLEY HOUSE, GARDINERS LANE, ASHWELL, HERTS.

ROBIN AND CATHERINE DUNLOP, THE GRANGE, ASHWELL, HERTS.

NORMAN AND JILL ELLIOTT, 12 FOX HILL ROAD, GUILDEN MORDEN, CAMBS.

BRENDA & REG FITZGERALD, "WESTLANDS", ASHWELL, HERTS.

ROBERT FOOTMAN, LORRAINE ELIZABETH FOOTMAN, ROBERT CHARLES FOOTMAN, 301 WEDON WAY, BYGRAVE, HERTS.

C. J. K. FORDHAM, ODSEY PARK, ASHWELL, HERTS.

A. J. FRANCIS, THE GUILD HOUSE, 55 HIGH STREET, ASHWELL, HERTS.

MR. AND MRS. J. F. GARROD, 99 COWSLIP HILL, LETCHWORTH, HERTS.

JENNY AND PETER JOHN GATES, 5 GREEN LANE, ASHWELL, HERTS.

CLIVE & CHRISTINA GODFREY, 43 WEST END, ASHWELL, HERTS.

SHEILA GRAHAM, 2 FORRESTERS COTTAGES, HIGH STREET, ASHWELL, HERTS.

MR. AND MRS. D. GROSSMAN, PILGRIMS COTTAGE, NEWNHAM, HERTS.

ERIC AND AUDREY GURNEY, ASHRIDGE FARM, ASHWELL, HERTS.

RON, ANNE, MARTIN & GEMMA HANCOCK, 51 ASHWELL STREET, ASHWELL, HERTS.

PETER & PAT HANKIN, 66 ASHWELL STREET, ASHWELL, HERTS.

WILLIAM HARDYMAN, 71 WOLVERLEY HOUSE, GARDINERS LANE, ASHWELL, HERTS.

MICHAEL WILLIAM HARDYMAN, 31 NURSERY CLOSE, BIGGLESWADE, BEDS.

KEITH WILLIAM HARDYMAN, 7 DYNES PLACE, MOGGERHANGER, BEDS.

GEOFF AND YVONNE HARPER, 22 WOODFORDE CLOSE, ASHWELL, HERTS.

L. & J. HARRINGTON, 9 NEW ROAD, GUILDEN MORDEN, CAMBS.

MRS. CHARLES HAYLOCK, LYNDHURST, ASHWELL, HERTS.

DR. & MRS. M. G. HOFFMAN, CHAPEL HOUSE, HINXWORTH, HERTS.

DOUGLAS AND BLANCHE HORSLEY, 15 NEWTOWN, TADLEY, BASINGSTOKE, HANTS.

GILLIAN GRAYLING HUMPHREYS, THE DORMERS, 19 LUCAS LANE, ASHWELL, HERTS.

BRIAN & JANET HUNT, 3 ANGELLS MEADOW, ASHWELL, HERTS.

MR. & MRS. A. I. HUNTER, 10 JUBILEE WAY, RUSSELL CLOSE, STEEPLE MORDEN, CAMBS.

MRS. GLADYS ILETT nee DANIELS, 16 BOGS GAP LANE, STEEPLE MORDEN, CAMBS.

JANE & GRAHAM IRVINE, AUSTRALIA.

TREVOR AND CHRIS JAMES, 56 BACK STREET, ASHWELL, HERTS.

VANESSA AND CLIFF JENKINSON, 10 WOODFORDE CLOSE, ASHWELL, HERTS.

MR. & MRS. A. R. KITELEY, GATLEY END FARM, STEEPLE MORDEN, CAMBS.

MR. & MRS. H. KRYPCZYK, LYNDA AND MARK, MANOR FARM, HINXWORTH, HERTS.

PAT & RAY LEACH, 'LAMBOURN', 33A CHURCH STREET, GUILDEN MORDEN, CAMBS.

MR. & MRS. M. D. LEARY, THE SCHOOL HOUSE, ODSEY, NR ASHWELL, HERTS.

RODNEY AND MARILYN LEETE, 53 ASHWELL STREET, ASHWELL, HERTS.

ROBIN AND EVE LIPSCOMBE, HUNT'S RIDGE, ASHWELL STREET, ASHWELL, HERTS.

DOUGLAS AND BETTY LOCKWOOD, 34 STATION ROAD, STEEPLE MORDEN, CAMBS.

MR. & MRS. J. LUNNESS, ROSE COTTAGE, STEEPLE MORDEN, CAMBS.

DAVID AND SUSAN MARSH, JAMES, CHRISTOPHER & HANNAH, SPRINGSIDE COTTAGE, 2 HIGH STREET, ASHWELL, HERTS.

ANDREW MARTINDALE, ABBOT'S HALL FARM HOUSE, AYLSHAM, NORFOLK.

MR. R. P. MITCHELL, 'HILLCREST', 1 NEW ROAD, GUILDEN MORDEN, CAMBS.

MR. T. J. MITCHELL, 15 WILBURY ROAD, LETCHWORTH, HERTS.

CAROL AND PETER MOORE, 25 DIXIES CLOSE, ASHWELL, HERTS.

VIV & MIKE MOORE, DIXIES FARMHOUSE, 91 HIGH STREET, ASHWELL, HERTS.

NICHOLAS AND JANE MOSS, THE OLD COTTAGE, HIGH STREET, ASHWELL, HERTS.

FERGUS AND LIZ MOYNIHAN, POPES FARM, EYEWORTH ROAD, ASHWELL, HERTS.

THE REV. AND MRS. JOHN MULLETT, 13 CHURCH LANE, MADINGLEY, CAMBS.

RICHARD AND CICELY MURFITT, 14 SILVER STREET, GUILDEN MORDEN, CAMBS.

JAMES D. NALLY, 21125 STONECROP PLACE, ASHBURN, VA 22011, USA.

MR. & MRS. B. NORTHERN, REDLANDS FARM, ASHWELL, HERTS.

VIV & VERA OLLEY, DIGSWELL MANOR, HIGH STREET, ASHWELL, HERTS.

MILDRED AND ERIC OSBORNE, 27 CHEYNEY STREET, STEEPLE MORDEN, CAMBS.

PATRICK OYSTON, MOBBS HOLE FARM, NORTHFIELDS ROAD, ASHWELL, HERTS.

ELSIE AND TONY OYSTON, 3 BUTTWAY, ASHWELL, HERTS.

JACK AND WINIFRED OYSTON, 77 STATION ROAD, ASHWELL, HERTS AND UNA DELLAR (NEE OYSTON), 3 BUXTONS LANE, GUILDEN MORDEN, CAMBS.

RUTH AND REG PAPWORTH, 10 COMMON ROAD, STOTFOLD, BEDS.

MR. A. PHIPPS, STOKE HOUSE FARM, STOKE HAMMOND.

GUY AND KAREN PICKETT, R.A.F.

JOHN AND JANE PICKETT, 8 PEACOCKS CLOSE, CAVENDISH, SUFFOLK.

LEO AND CHRISTINE PICKETT, 'CHAKRATA', 3 NEWNHAM WAY, ASHWELL, HERTS.

MR. & MRS. W. J. A. PORTEOUS, 73 BACK STREET, ASHWELL, HERTS.

MR. & MRS. A. G. POTTER, LABURNHAM COTTAGE, 50 STATION ROAD, ASHWELL, HERTS.

CAROLE ANN PRIESTLEY, HINXWORTH PLACE, HINXWORTH, HERTS.

JOHN & SHEILA PRYKE, VENTNOR HOUSE, HIGH STREET, ASHWELL, HERTS.

NORA REEVES, 9 LUCAS LANE, ASHWELL, HERTS.

SUE AND DAI ROWLEY-JONES, WORLANDS, ASHWELL STREET, ASHWELL, HERTS.

MATTHEW ROWNTREE, ASH COTTAGE, 10 GARDINERS LANE, ASHWELL, HERTS.

DERRICK AND DENISE SEABY, 64 BEDFORD ROAD, HITCHIN, HERTS.

BYRON & FAY SEARLE, 18 DIXIES CLOSE, ASHWELL, HERTS.

ROBERT SHELDRICK, 29 MILL STREET, ASHWELL, HERTS.

SUZANNE SHELDRICK, LETCHWORTH, HERTS.

JONATHAN SHEPPARD, WEST GROVE, PENNSYLVANIA, USA.

GURNEY SHEPPARD, ASHWELL BURY.

DENIS JOHN SIMMONS, 68 ASHWELL STREET, ASHWELL, HERTS.

ALISON PULLAR STAFFORD, "THE CUCKOO", ASHWELL, HERTS.

MRS. ELIZABETH M. STONE, 18 WOODFORDE CLOSE, ASHWELL, HERTS.

MRS. E. STURGESS, 16 GREATFELLING FIELD, MARY TAVY, DEVON.

ROBERT SWAIN, 32 HODWELL, ASHWELL, HERTS.

GRAHAM & SHEILA SWALLOW, 87 BACK STREET, ASHWELL, HERTS.

HAMISH SYMINGTON, 2 BOGS GAP LANE, STEEPLE MORDEN, CAMBS.

EILEEN & JOHN TEN HOVE, 11 ANGELLS MEADOW, ASHWELL, HERTS.

MR. & MRS. I. THOMAS, NEXT ODSEY, STATION ROAD, ASHWELL, HERTS.

JEAN AND ERIC TODD, 14 WOODFORDE CLOSE, ASHWELL, HERTS.

STEVEN & ANNE TOLLEY, 33 HIGH STREET, ASHWELL, HERTS.

MRS. BESSIE WALLACE, SALE'S ACRE, ASHWELL, HERTS.

MR. & MRS. JOHN & FRANCES WALTON, THE OLD STABLES, 124 STATION ROAD, ODSEY, HERTS.

DAVID WARD, 17 BRITANNIA AVENUE, WHITSTABLE, KENT.

PAULINE WHITBY, 9 MILL STREET, ASHWELL, HERTS.

ALAN & ROSEMARY WHITE, 93 STATION ROAD, ASHWELL, HERTS.

MRS. ISABEL WILES, "WELLESBOURNE", HIGH STREET, ASHWELL, HERTS.

CHRIS WILKINS, HIGH STREET, SHEFFORD, BEDS.

DAWN & RODERICK WINTERHALDER, 5 SILVER STREET, ASHWELL, HERTS.

DON & MARY WRIGHT, 26 MONKS RISE, WELWYN GARDEN CITY, HERTS.